GO STRESS FREE

HAPPINESS. PEACE. SERENITY

DR JAWAHAR SURISETTI

LAUNCHPAD

An imprint of
Srishti Publishers & Distributors

Srishti Publishers & Distributors
A unit of AJR Publishing LLP
212A, Peacock Lane, Shahpur Jat,
New Delhi – 110 049
editorial@srishtipublishers.com

First Published by Launchpad,
an imprint of Srishti Publishers & Distributors in 2025

10 9 8 7 6 5 4 3 2 1

This is a work of non-fiction based on the author's research about the subject. While due care has been taken by the author and publisher to verify contents at press time, any inadvertent miss that is brought to their notice shall be duly verified and updated subsequently.

Printed and bound in India.

Contents

Introduction: A Journey from Stress to Serenity

In the midst of a world that seems to be spinning faster and faster, with endless demands and distractions pulling us in every direction, stress has become a universal language – a shared experience that crosses all boundaries of age, culture, and background. Whether we are juggling the demands of work and family, navigating the challenges of relationships and health, or simply trying to find our way in an uncertain world, stress is a constant companion, a shadow that follows us wherever we go.

For many of us, stress has become so familiar that we barely even notice it anymore. It is the background noise of our lives, the static that fills our minds and bodies with tension and unease. We may feel like we are coping, like we are handling the pressures of modern life with grace and resilience. But beneath the surface, stress takes its toll

– eroding our physical health, our emotional well-being, and our sense of connection to ourselves and others.

The cost of this chronic stress is staggering. Studies have linked prolonged stress to a wide range of health problems, from heart disease and diabetes to anxiety and depression. Stress weakens our immune system, disrupts our sleep, and interferes with our ability to think clearly and make good decisions. It strains our relationships, leaving us feeling isolated and alone. And it robs us of our joy and vitality, leaving us feeling exhausted and overwhelmed by the demands of daily life.

But what if there was another way? What if we could learn to navigate the challenges of life with greater ease and grace, to find a sense of inner peace and clarity even in the midst of chaos and uncertainty? What if we could cultivate a deeper connection to ourselves and others, a sense of purpose and meaning that transcends the stresses and struggles of the world around us?

This is the promise of "*Go Stress Free: Happiness. Peace. Serenity.*" In this groundbreaking book, we explore the roots of stress and the path to lasting peace, drawing on the latest research in psychology, neuroscience, and spirituality. We offer a roadmap for personal and collective transformation, a guide to living with greater authenticity, compassion, and joy in a world that often feels overwhelming and out of control.

At the heart of this book is a simple but profound insight: that stress is not an inevitable fact of life, but a reflection of our relationship to ourselves and the world around us. When we are disconnected from our deepest values and aspirations, when we are caught up in patterns of fear and resistance, stress is the natural result. But when we learn to align ourselves with our true nature, to cultivate mindfulness, compassion, and connection, we discover a wellspring of inner peace and resilience that is always available to us.

This insight is not new. For centuries, wisdom traditions around the world have pointed to the possibility of living with greater ease and harmony, of finding a sense of grace and purpose in the midst of life's challenges. From the teachings of the Buddha to the insights of modern psychology, there is a rich lineage of knowledge and practice that can guide us on the path to greater well-being and fulfilment.

What is new is the way that this book brings together these diverse perspectives into a cohesive and accessible framework for personal and societal transformation. Drawing on the work of thought leaders as well as cutting-edge research in fields like positive psychology and neuroscience, "*Go Stress Free: Happiness. Peace. Serenity*" offers a comprehensive and practical guide to living with greater mindfulness, compassion, and purpose in the modern world.

The book is organized into ten chapters, each exploring a different facet of the journey from stress to serenity. In Chapter 1, we delve into the roots of stress, examining how our evolutionary history and modern culture conspire to keep us trapped in cycles of fear and reactivity. We explore the impact of chronic stress on our bodies, minds, and relationships, and make the case for a new paradigm of stress resilience and transformation.

In Chapters 2-4, we explore the inner landscape of the mind and how our thoughts, beliefs, and stories shape our experience of stress and well-being. We learn about the power of mindfulness and self-awareness to interrupt patterns of negative thinking and cultivate greater clarity and focus. We also explore the role of self-compassion and acceptance in healing the wounds of the past and embracing the fullness of the present moment.

Chapters 5-7 focus on the importance of connection and community in building stress resilience and well-being. We explore the science of social support and the power of authentic communication to deepen our relationships and create a sense of belonging and purpose. We also examine the role of empathy and compassion in building bridges of understanding across differences, and the potential for collective healing and transformation.

In Chapters 8-9, we turn our attention to the body and the natural world, exploring how mindful movement, nutrition, and time in nature can help us cultivate greater vitality, creativity, and joy. We learn about the science of the relaxation response and the power of the breath to calm the mind and regulate the nervous system. We also explore the role of play, laughter, and letting go in releasing the grip of stress and cultivating a sense of lightness and ease.

Finally, in Chapter 10, we integrate all of these insights and practices into a holistic vision of stress resilience and transformation, one that honours the interconnectedness of mind, body, and spirit. We explore the power of purpose and meaning to give our lives direction and significance, and the potential for personal and societal awakening in the face of the challenges of our time.

Throughout the book, we include practical exercises, case studies, and personal stories to illustrate the key concepts and make them accessible and applicable to daily life. We also draw on the latest research and data to support our insights and recommendations, providing a solid foundation of evidence-based practices for stress management and well-being.

The author of "*Go Stress Free: Happiness. Peace. Serenity*" is Dr. Jawahar Surisetti, a psychologist and futurist with over two decades of experience in the field of stress resilience and well-being. Dr. Surisetti has worked with thousands of individuals and organizations around the world, helping them cultivate greater mindfulness, compassion, and purpose in the face of life's challenges.

In addition to his seminal work, Dr. Surisetti is a renowned researcher and thought leader in the field of stress and well-being. He has published numerous articles and books on the science of mindfulness and compassion, and has been featured in leading media outlets such as The New York Times, The Washington Post, and NPR.

Dr. Surisetti's approach to stress and well-being is grounded in a deep understanding of the human condition, as well as a commitment to social justice and collective healing. He believes that the path to personal and societal transformation is one that requires both inner work and outer action, a willingness to confront the root causes of stress and suffering while also cultivating the inner resources of mindfulness, compassion, and resilience.

In writing "*Go Stress Free: Happiness. Peace. Serenity*" Dr. Surisetti has drawn on his extensive experience and research to create a comprehensive and accessible guide to stress resilience and well-being. He has collaborated with leading experts in fields such as psychology, neuroscience, and contemplative practice to ensure that the book is grounded in the latest scientific evidence and practical wisdom.

At the same time, Dr. Surisetti has brought his own personal journey and insights to the book, sharing stories and reflections from his own life and practice. He believes that the path to serenity is one that requires both knowledge and experience, a willingness to learn from the wisdom of others while also trusting in the wisdom of our own hearts and minds.

The result is a book that is both deeply informative and profoundly transformative, a guide to living with greater ease, purpose, and joy in a world that often feels overwhelming and uncertain. Whether you are a seasoned practitioner of mindfulness and compassion or simply someone looking for a way to navigate the challenges of daily life with greater grace and resilience, "*Go Stress Free: Happiness. Peace. Serenity*" offers a pathway to lasting peace and well-being.

As Dr. Surisetti writes in the introduction, "This book is an invitation to a different way of being in the world, a way that is grounded in mindfulness, compassion, and connection. It is a call to wake up to the beauty and possibility of the present moment, to embrace the fullness of our humanity with all its joys and sorrows. And it is a reminder that we are not alone on this journey, that we are part of a larger web of life that sustains and supports us, even in the darkest of times."

In a world that often feels fragmented and disconnected, "*Go Stress Free: Happiness. Peace. Serenity*" offers a vision of wholeness and integration, a way of living that honours the deep interconnectedness of all things. It is a book that challenges us to look beyond the surface of our lives and to discover the deeper truth of who we are and what we are capable of becoming.

Whether you are seeking to reduce stress, cultivate greater mindfulness and compassion, or simply find a sense of peace and purpose in a chaotic world, this book is a valuable resource and guide. It is a testament to the power of the human spirit to transform suffering into wisdom, to find grace and beauty in the midst of life's challenges.

As you embark on this journey from stress to serenity, know that you are not alone. You are part of a growing community of individuals and organizations around the world who are committed to creating a more mindful, compassionate, and sustainable way of living. By cultivating these qualities in ourselves and in our communities, we have the power to create ripples of positive change that extend far beyond our individual lives.

So let us begin this journey together, with open hearts and minds, ready to embrace the full spectrum of human experience with courage, compassion, and grace. Let us learn from the wisdom of those who have gone before us, while also trusting in the wisdom of our own inner guidance. And let us remember that the path to serenity is not a destination, but a way of being in the world, a commitment to living with greater presence, purpose, and joy, moment by moment, day by day.

1
The Roots of Stress

There once was a zebra grazing peacefully in the savanna. Suddenly, a lion leapt out from the tall grass in an attack. Instantly, a surge of energy shot through the zebra's body – heart racing, muscles tensed, senses heightened. In a flash, it bolted away to safety, stress response activated to preserve its life.

For us humans, the threats have changed, but the same primal wiring governs our nervous system. While we don't typically face predators, the challenges of our modern concrete jungles – traffic jams, work deadlines, financial pressures, relationship conflicts, 24/7 digital demands – trigger our "fight, flight or freeze" response just the same. Physiologically, we often react as if our life were endangered, even when it's not.

Chronic activation of stress, without the resolution our distant ancestors experienced after fleeing or fighting, has become the new normal. Stress is now a constant, low-grade hum, like an ambient noise we barely notice... until it crescendos into a painful roar we cannot ignore.

The Stress Epidemic

Make no mistake, we're in the midst of a global stress epidemic. The World Health Organization has declared stress the "health epidemic of the 21st century." Ubiquitous and mounting stress is evident in sobering statistics:

- 80 per cent of workers feel stress on the job, nearly half say they need help in learning how to manage stress, and 42 per cent say their coworkers need such help (American Institute of Stress)
- 75 per cent of adults reported experiencing moderate to high levels of stress in the past month, and nearly half reported that their stress has increased in the past year (American Psychological Association)
- Stress causes nearly 1 million workers to miss work every day, and up to 80 per cent of workplace accidents (American Institute of Stress)
- Stress is the basic cause of 60 per cent of all human illness and disease (American Institute of Stress)
- 3 out of four doctor's visits are for stress-related ailments (American Institute of Stress)

The toll of stress is pervasive and profound, deteriorating physical health, mental well-being, relationships, productivity, and quality of life. Stress is a complex, many-headed hydra – and to truly gain victory over it, we must understand how it works within us.

The Anatomy of Stress

What exactly is this force that exerts such a potent effect on our bodies and minds? At its essence, stress is a neurochemical cascade meant to help us survive. When we perceive a threat, whether real or imagined, the amygdala, the primal part of our brain governing survival instincts, signals an alarm.

This triggers the sympathetic nervous system to flood the body with stress hormones like cortisol and adrenaline. Pupils dilate, heartbeat quickens, blood pressure rises, and breath speeds up. Nutrients and oxygen rush to major muscles, preparing us to fight or flee. Higher thought in the prefrontal cortex shuts down as primal instincts take over in a laser focus on survival.

This mobilization of resources is brilliant for escaping acute danger. But when activated chronically, without physical resolution, it turns toxic. Persistently elevated cortisol leads to impaired cognition, blood sugar imbalances, weight gain, heart disease, impaired immunity, and more. Prolonged sympathetic nervous system activation causes emotional reactivity, anxiety, depression, and burnout.

Over time, the cumulative effect is akin to revving a car engine incessantly without ever shifting into drive. The gears grind, the engine overheats, and steam pours out from the hood. Eventually, the inevitable happens – it breaks down. And so do we.

Our distant ancestors faced occasional bouts of acute stress during predator attacks or hunts. But in between, they had long stretches of time in the parasympathetic state – the "rest and digest" mode, where the body restores itself.

In contrast, our stress is constant and complex, caused not by literal lions but by psychological threats to our esteem, identity, sense of belonging, or future security. It's not a discrete moment of danger but an endless onslaught of demands, pressures, and rapid change. Our primal physiology can't tell the difference between an attacking lion and a looming deadline – it responds the same.

The Pace of Modern Life

In many ways, modern life itself has become a threat to our prehistoric biology. In the span of a few generations, we've seen an unprecedented acceleration of technology, information, social change, and stimulation that far exceeds the nervous system's evolved capacity. We now live life at a dizzying velocity, powered by a 24/7 stream of digital pings and perpetual pressure to perform.

Our hunter-gatherer ancestors lived by the rising and setting of the sun, perfectly attuned to nature's timeless rhythms. Their work was in tune with their biology. In contrast, we live largely divorced from the organic rhythms of nature, attuned instead to clocks, calendars, and economic demands. The pace of our lives has accelerated far beyond what our primal minds and bodies were meant to handle.

In this age of perpetual overload, no one is immune to stress. No matter what corner of the earth we inhabit, from sprawling cities to serene villages, we all feel the effects of speeding beyond our physiological speed limit. Most of us are stressed not because we choose to be but because, in our lightning-paced, ever-changing landscape, it takes tremendous intention not to be.

A World of Perception

At its root, stress is about perception. Nothing has meaning except the meaning we give it. What one person experiences as unbearably stressful, another might experience as invigorating. The determining factor is not the situation itself but the way in which we perceive, interpret, and respond to it.

Consider public speaking, for example. One oft-cited poll found that the average person fears public speaking more than death itself. Standing in front of a crowd, prepared to bare your knowledge and passion, can feel like stepping before a firing squad, heart slamming like a prisoner awaiting the firing shot.

Yet those same sensations – racing heart, sweaty palms, heightened alertness – would be interpreted entirely differently by someone who saw the situation as an exciting opportunity to share their passion. Objectively, the circumstances are identical. But the subjective interpretation completely alters the experience. As Shakespeare poetically phrased it: "There is nothing either good or bad, but thinking makes it so."

This points to a fundamental truth about stress – it's not an objective force outside of us but something that is constructed through our perceptions and reactions. No doubt, there are real external pressures. But it's the way we interpret those pressures through the filter of our beliefs, expectations, and assumptions that creates our inner experience.

The Expectations Trap

So much stress comes from shoulds and supposed tos. From cultural conditioning about who we should be, what we should achieve, how we should live and relate.

We internalize an image of success and acceptability that's often not our own. The further out of alignment we live from our authentic essence, the more stressed and constricted we feel.

Instead of pursuing goals that resonate deeply with our true selves, we pursue what we think we should based on external expectations. We strive to have the relationship, career, income, body, house, and status that we've been taught equate to success and happiness. Pushing harder and harder with a grim determination, running faster on a treadmill to nowhere.

But no matter what we attain, the underlying angst remains because we're chasing a mirage. The goals aren't rooted in our own truth. We've absorbed images of success and happiness from family, media, culture, and projected future fantasies that often have little to do with our core, authentic desires. We live imprisoned by expectations, mostly unconscious, of who we imagine we should be.

This is stress on steroids: living in constant comparison and lack. A rampant virus robbing a whole society of presence, fulfilment, and joy. We become human doings instead of human beings, addicted to external validation while becoming disconnected from our inner well of peace and wholeness.

If we have the courage to drill into the core of stress, we see it's a crisis of meaning. The very way we've structured and paced our lives leads to existential anxiety. Lost and distanced from our innermost nature, we feel at odds with existence itself, waging an unwinnable struggle to wrest peace from someplace outside ourselves.

The Gifts of Stress

Indeed, stress whispers a vital message, if only we'll listen. It tells us something essential is out of balance and urges us back into alignment. Stress isn't an obstacle to growth and fulfilment but an invitation to it. The discomfort we feel is the soul's call to evolve, a powerful impetus to look inward and question our conditioned patterns.

Seen in this light, stress is not a burden but a blessing, not a problem to solve but a profound teacher. It points to the places where we've gotten stuck, where we've veered from our authentic path, where we've hitched our well-being to transient things. It calls us to awaken, to live and work with integrity, to relate with openhearted presence, to honour what's truly important. Stress, when faced consciously, can be a catalyst for growth and transformation.

But for this to be possible, we must change our relationship with stress from adversary to ally. No longer running, repressing, or masking our stress, but attending to it with self-compassionate curiosity. The way out of stress is not more struggle, gritted teeth and steely resolve, but a softening into acceptance. By bringing a gentle, caring presence to our felt experience, the contracted stress response can't help but unwind and release.

The journey toward a less stressed life begins with acknowledging that in this accelerated age, stress is inevitable...and that's okay. When we demand a life free from stress, we layer more tension on top of the stress itself. But when we can gaze upon it through the gentle eyes of acceptance, we gain access to the calm that was there all along beneath the surface agitation.

The great spiritual teacher Krishnamurti was once asked how he remained so peaceful amidst life's turmoil. "Do you want to know my secret?" he replied. "I don't mind what happens." There's immense freedom in that – not fighting with reality but surrendering into the spaciousness of the present moment beyond conditions.

Ultimately, stress is an inside job. It comes from demanding that reality be different from what it is. Peace comes from making peace with what is, recognizing that every situation, no matter how challenging, contains a hidden gift, a potential for awakening and transformation. When we learn to surf the waves of life instead of resisting them, we reclaim our inherent power to choose our inner state.

The Possibility of Peace

Make no mistake – this is not a path for the faint of heart. It's a warrior's quest that takes tremendous intention, discipline, and courage. To find equanimity amidst the whirlpool of modern life demands a conscious and constant practice, swimming upstream against the cultural currents of angst and acquisition. It's a radical reclaiming of responsibility for our own well-being from the inside out.

Yet for those willing to heed the call and venture inward, immense rewards await – the lived experience of unconditional well-being, presence, and authentic self-expression. Though the stresses of life may not change, we have the capacity to forge an unshakeable core of inner calm that meets whatever arises. When we stop waiting for external circumstances to align, we liberate ourselves into the perfection of the moment.

The fact that you hold this book in your hands is an invitation to this journey. It's an opportunity to examine your conditioned patterns around stress and chart a new course. Throughout these pages, we'll explore holistic strategies for transformation, spanning mindset, lifestyle, practices, and purpose. By weaving together ancient wisdom and modern psychology, you'll receive an integral roadmap for creating a stress-resilient life aligned with your deepest truth.

Through concrete teachings and experiential exercises, you'll learn how to:

- Respond instead of react to stressors, becoming a master of your inner world
- Move from resistance to curiosity, tension to self-compassion, anxiety into presence
- Gain clarity of mind through reflective practices
- Cultivate physiological calm and energetic attunement
- Nurture stress-releasing relationships and support systems
- Design a lifestyle and work aligned with your natural rhythms
- Connect to the transcendent peace of your core essence

The journey through these pages is an invitation to more than stress relief – it's an invitation to a whole new way of being alive. One that's fully present, heartfelt, purposeful and free. An existence not at odds with life but in love with it. A way of meeting each moment that recognizes the perfection in what is, even as it flows into what's becoming. It's a path of awakening to your most magnificent self, a self too spacious for stress to overshadow.

The journey begins now. May it bring you home to the vast calm that was always there, waiting patiently beneath the surface chatter of the stressed mind. May it awaken you to the beauty and bounty of this very moment, the only moment we ever have. And may it reconnect you to your innate wellspring of peace, power, and potential to create the life that your soul yearns for.

The Roots of Stress – Practical Takeaways

Understanding Modern Stress

1. While our stress response evolved to handle acute physical threats, we now face chronic psychological stressors that our biology isn't designed for:
   * Work deadlines
   * Financial pressures
   * Digital overwhelm
   * Relationship conflicts
   * Constant connectivity

2. The stress epidemic is evidenced by alarming statistics:
   * 80 per cent of workers feel workplace stress
   * 75 per cent of adults report moderate to high stress levels
   * 60 per cent of human illness and disease is stress-related
   * 3 out of four doctor's visits are stress-related

The Biology of Stress

1. The stress response triggers a cascade of physiological changes:
   * Release of cortisol and adrenaline
   * Increased heart rate and blood pressure
   * Faster breathing
   * Redirected blood flow to major muscles
   * Suppressed higher-level thinking

2. While this response is helpful for acute danger, chronic activation leads to:
   * Impaired cognition
   * Blood sugar imbalances
   * Weight gain
   * Heart disease
   * Compromised immunity
   * Emotional instability

Key Insights About Stress

1. Stress is primarily about perception:
   * The same situation can be stressful or invigorating, depending on our interpretation
   * Our thoughts and beliefs shape our stress response more than external circumstances
   * We have the power to change our relationship with stress

2. Much stress comes from misaligned expectations:
   * Cultural conditioning about who we "should" be
   * Pursuing goals that don't reflect our authentic desires
   * Living by external standards rather than internal truth
   * Constant comparison and perceived lack

Transforming Your Relationship with Stress

1. View stress as information:
   * It signals when something is out of alignment
   * It can be a catalyst for growth and transformation
   * It points to areas needing attention and care

2. Practice acceptance:
   * Fighting stress creates more tension
   * Acknowledge that some stress is inevitable in modern life
   * Meet stress with curiosity rather than resistance

Action Steps for Moving Forward

1. Begin noticing your stress triggers:
   * Track situations that activate your stress response
   * Observe your typical reactions and patterns
   * Notice the thoughts and beliefs underlying your stress

2. Start cultivating stress awareness:
    * Check in with your body throughout the day
    * Notice physical signs of stress activation
    * Practice pausing before reacting to stressors

3. Implement basic stress management:
    * Take regular breaks from digital devices
    * Schedule time for rest and recovery
    * Maintain consistent sleep patterns
    * Move your body regularly
    * Practice conscious breathing

Remember: While we can't eliminate all stress, we can change our relationship with it and develop greater resilience. The journey begins with awareness and a willingness to explore new ways of responding to life's challenges.

2
The Illusion of Control

Once upon a time, in a bustling village at the foot of a great mountain, there lived a man named Siddhartha. Siddhartha was known throughout the land for his unshakeable serenity. No matter what challenges or turmoil arose, he maintained a beatific smile and radiant presence.

The villagers were perplexed by Siddhartha's unrelenting calm. They couldn't understand how he navigated life with such ease while they felt perpetually stressed and struggling. One day, driven by desperation, they gathered around Siddhartha and pleaded, "Please, wise one, tell us the secret to your peace."

Siddhartha gazed at the crowd with compassion and replied, "Dear friends, there is no secret. I have simply realized the futility of trying to control that which is beyond my control. When we demand that life unfold according to our plans, we suffer. When we surrender to the great unfolding, we find freedom."

The villagers looked perplexed. Control was the only way they knew. Letting go seemed foreign, even frightening. Seeing their confusion, Siddhartha continued:

"Think of the farmer who toils day and night to control his crop. He frets over the weather, the pests, and the soil. He exhausts himself trying to bend every condition to his will. But in the end, all his efforts cannot make the seed grow or the rain fall. He cannot control the yield, only the effort he puts in. The wise farmer plants the fields, then surrenders the outcome to nature's hand."

The Illusion of Certainty

Siddhartha's parable points to a pervasive human struggle: our desperate attempt to control life. We cling to the illusion that if we just plan enough, work hard enough, worry long enough, we can bend reality to our will and guarantee the outcomes we desire. Uncertainty feels dangerous, like standing at the edge of an abyss, so we scramble for terra firma – something to hold on to and be sure of.

But the truth is, the only certainty in life is uncertainty. No amount of control can predetermine the shifting tides of existence. We live in a universe that's fundamentally unpredictable – from the quantum foam to the weather next week to how our lives will ultimately unfold. French philosopher Voltaire phrased it poetically: "Doubt is not a pleasant condition, but certainty is an absurd one."

Yet we don't need to venture into the realms of particle physics or meteorology to recognize the folly of certainty – our everyday experiences make it plain. We pour tremendous energy into mapping out our lives, setting goals, and striving for a predictable future. But as the Yiddish proverb sagely puts it, "Man makes plans...and God laughs." Again and again, we're blindsided by unexpected events that shake our notion of a controllable world.

Still, we resist surrendering our illusions because they provide a fragile sense of safety. We believe that if we just amass enough knowledge, skill, wealth, or status, we'll be able to control our destiny. But in clinging to this belief, we live in a perpetual state of stress and tension, bracing against the inevitable tides of change.

The Stress of Control

The need for control is a core driver of stress. When we're attached to a particular outcome, we live in fear of not attaining it. Our mind gets trapped in an endless loop of rehearsing what might go wrong, trying to preempt every possible pitfall. We get so fixated on the destination that we miss the journey entirely.

You can see this play out in all arenas of life. The parent who hovers over their child's every move, terrified of any misstep or failure. The manager who micromanages every project is unable to trust the process. The perfectionist who procrastinates endlessly, paralyzed by the need to get it "just right." The treadmill of striving for control leads straight to anxiety, burnout, and missing out on life.

The Buddha recognized this human proclivity over 2500 years ago. The root of suffering, he taught, is attachment: the mind's sticky tendency to grasp onto an outcome, a circumstance, an identity. We get hooked on an idea of how things should be, then feel incessant dissatisfaction because reality has other plans. In Buddha's words, "Peace comes from within. Do not seek it without."

Surrender ≠ Resignation

Now, this wisdom can easily be misinterpreted as a call for resignation, apathy, or helplessness. But accepting uncertainty is not the same as descending into passivity or victimhood. Surrender is not succumbing to life but attuning and aligning with it. In the words of contemporary spiritual teacher Adyashanti, "Surrender is not a weakness, it is strength. It takes tremendous strength to surrender life to the supreme, to the cosmic unfolding."

The aim is not to relinquish agency but to deploy our energy intelligently. Instead of exhausting ourselves paddling against the current of what is, we navigate life with wisdom, focusing on what we can influence and releasing what we cannot. As theologian Reinhold Niebuhr summarized in the poignant Serenity Prayer: "God, grant me the serenity to accept the things I cannot change, the courage to change the things I can, and the wisdom to know the difference."

The art of living skillfully means discerning this pivotal difference. To be sure, there's much within our sphere of control: our thoughts, interpretations, choices, actions, and attitudes. But the broader circumstances of existence – forces of nature, other people's behaviours, the economy, global events – remain forever beyond our command. Serenity comes from focusing our energy on the former and making peace with the latter.

Trapped on the Hedonic Treadmill

Why then do we strive so desperately for control if it's ultimately futile? A core reason is that we've been conditioned to believe our happiness depends on it. At the heart of the struggle for control is a simple assumption: "When I get X, I'll feel Y." When I get the relationship, job, house, income, approval, or achievement, then I'll feel content, successful, and at peace.

But this belief keeps us trapped on what psychologists call the "hedonic treadmill" – an endless pursuit of the next hit of gratification. We're perpetually waiting for a future moment to finally feel ok, while our actual life passes by unlived. Even when we get what we want, the satisfaction is short-lived before we fixate on the next goal post. It's a recipe for chronic stress and existential angst.

The truth is, no external attainment can provide the unconditional peace we yearn for. Nothing outside ourselves—no circumstance, possession, or validation—can grant unshakeable inner tranquillity. That's simply not how the mind works. Lasting contentment is an inside job that demands relinquishing the mind's addiction to control.

The Gifts of Surrender

What becomes possible when we release the steel grip of control? When do we stop fighting the river of life and allow ourselves to flow with the current? A profound shift occurs – from a life of striving and stress to one of presence, spontaneity, and true aliveness. When the illusion of control drops away, we discover the immensity of our being that's untouched by transient circumstances.

Suddenly, we're available to the beauty and bounty of the moment. No longer fixated on controlling the next experience, we can savour the one we're having. Presence flows through us, transforming mundane moments into treasures beyond measure. Little things – a crisp breeze, a child's laugh, the scent of jasmine – awaken us to the miracle of being alive in a way the busy mind can never touch.

Furthermore, when we align ourselves with life's intrinsic uncertainty, we tap into immense creativity and adaptability. Instead of being rigid and reactive, we become fluid and responsive. We develop pliancy of attention – the capacity to meet each moment freshly instead of imposing our agendas. This, in turn, makes us more effective, as we bring openness and curiosity to each situation instead of a white-knuckle drive for results.

The irony is, when we relinquish the illusion of control, we actually gain more influence. We're able to respond intelligently to what's needed, pivoting gracefully as new information arises. Not needing circumstances to be a certain way, we navigate them with wisdom and equanimity. Like a martial artist who harnesses the opponent's energy instead of opposing it head-on, we collaborate with life's unfolding instead of struggling against it.

Embracing Groundlessness

Ultimately, letting go of control invites us to embrace the groundlessness of existence. To recognize that the very ground we stand on is forever shifting, all forms forever dissolving back into primordial flux. Though the ego finds this terrifying, always grasping for a fixed identity, the soul rejoices in the freedom it offers. In the words of Sufi mystic Rumi: "Let yourself be silently drawn by the strange pull of what you really love. It will not lead you astray."

Indeed, embracing groundlessness connects us with the very source of life - the vast creative intelligence from which all forms arise. Beyond our individual will, there's a higher wisdom always at work, ceaselessly bringing forth the universe in its wild, unprecedented glory. Our stressed and doubting minds may not always perceive it. But when we surrender to the flow of what is, we come into profound harmony with this intelligence.

The 13th-century mystic Meister Eckhart poetically captured this recognition: "The eye with which I see God is the same eye with which God sees me." In other words, beneath the surface waves of control and chaos is an oceanic Oneness that permeates and provides for all. Our task is to attune ourselves with this primordial unity, to relax into the perfection of the moment exactly as it is.

From this vantage point, life ceases to be a problem to solve and instead becomes an adventure to be lived.

No longer at odds with the ceaseless flow of change, we relinquish our psychological defences and open to the fullness of experience – pleasure and pain, gain and loss, birth and death. We hold our plans and goals lightly, taking inspired action while releasing attachment to outcomes. Like the Zen archer who focuses on the target but relinquishes the need to hit the bullseye, we bring commitment to our aims but spaciousness to the results.

Practices for Presence

This all sounds beautiful in theory, but how do we actually embody it? How do we concretely practice relinquishing control and relaxing into the flow of life? There are myriad methods, stemming from the wisdom of diverse spiritual traditions. At their core, they all share one aim: to bring us out of the stressed, striving mind and into the spaciousness of the present.

Mindfulness is one foundational approach – the practice of bringing non-judgmental awareness to our moment-to-moment experience. Through methods like meditation, yoga, tai chi, and breath work, we cultivate the capacity to observe our racing thoughts and reactive patterns without getting hooked by them. We learn to drop out of the mind stream and into the sensory aliveness of the Now.

Another key practice is self-inquiry – turning attention inward to investigate the nature of the self. By posing the question "Who am I?", we see through the mind's limited self-concepts and touch a dimension of pure being that's prior to control. Methods like journaling, psychotherapy, and silent retreats support this process of self-discovery.

Communion with nature is also a potent portal to presence. Away from the frenetic distractions of technology and to-do lists, we sync up with more organic, unhurried rhythms. The patient unfolding of a flower, the graceful lilt of a songbird, the dreamlike drifting of clouds – all of these remind us of a natural order that proceeds effortlessly, without stress. In nature, we can't help but release our grandiose illusions of control as we marvel at powers so much vaster than our own.

At the deepest level, surrendering control means consecrating our lives in service of the sacred. When we align ourselves with a transcendent source and offer our actions for the highest good, we access a profound stream of synchronicity that orchestrates our lives better than the ego ever could. This alignment demands deep listening – attuning to our inner compass, the soul's intuitive guidance on which way to go. No longer trying to control life, we let ourselves be danced by the Infinite – an exhilaratingly vulnerable position that opens us to unprecedented miracles.

Conclusion

Dear reader, I invite you into the radical possibility of a life beyond control. A life of pure presence and spiritual surrender, of deep trust in the intelligence of the Whole. Through the practices and principles in this chapter, you can progressively unwind the stressful patterns of your mind and discover the vast calm of your Essential Nature. This isn't a linear path, but a moment-to-moment choice – to release your demand for life to be a certain way and open to the perfection of what is.

As you walk this path, you will likely encounter resistance. The ego will kick and scream, desperate to maintain the illusion of control. Loved ones may not understand your new way of being. Old habit patterns will resurface, tempting you back into anxious striving. This is all normal and natural. The journey of awakening is not a perfect forward march, but a Coyote path of twists, turns, and humbling reversals.

But when the resistance arises, I invite you to meet it with great compassion. Trying to fight or control our protective patterns only creates more stress. The key is welcoming everything – every fear, doubt, and stressful sensation – in the warm embrace of your attention. Each triggered arising becomes an opportunity to practice loving what is, disrupting the ancient habit of rejecting the present moment.

Ultimately, this path beyond control is one of immense humility. Of bowing before the wondrous intricacy of the universe, recognizing we can never grasp it all through our finite minds. It's a path of ego relaxation, of surrendering our self-will into the higher hands of Grace. We become the hollow flute through which the Infinite plays its tune – a 'Thy Will be done rather than a My will be done.

Through this lens, stress ceases to be an enemy and instead becomes a compassionate teacher, revealing where we're caught in resistance, where we're clinging to control. Each stressor becomes a mirror, inviting us into deeper acceptance and trust. In the bittersweet ache of uncertainty, we take refuge in the intimacy of the here and now, knowing it's the only true home we can ever have.

So as you turn these pages, I pray you come to know the unshakeable peace that's always and already here, prior to control. The peace of pure presence, of resting in the Eye of the Storm, no matter how loud the winds howl. May you discover a profound surrender into the Holy Mystery of each moment, into the love that moves the sun and stars. Let us practice together, with infinite compassion, as we relinquish control and come home to life's stunning immediacy.

The Illusion of Control – Practical Takeaways

Understanding Control

1. Recognize what you can and cannot control:
   * Within your control: thoughts, choices, actions, responses
   * Beyond your control: others' behaviour, natural events, most outcomes
   * Focus energy on your sphere of influence rather than external circumstances

Notice control patterns:

* Identify where you struggle to let go
* Observe how control attempts increase stress
* Notice physical tension associated with controlling behaviour

Breaking Free from the Control Cycle

1. Practice acceptance:
   * Acknowledge uncertainty as natural
   * Allow events to unfold without resistance
   * Distinguish between acceptance and resignation

2. Release outcome attachment:
   * Set intentions while holding goals lightly
   * Focus on process over results
   * Celebrate effort regardless of outcome

Practical Mindfulness Techniques

1. Daily mindfulness practices:
    * Start with 5-10 minutes of meditation
    * Practice mindful breathing during stress
    * Use nature walks for present-moment awareness
    * Observe thoughts without getting caught in them

2. Body-based awareness:
    * Regular body scans to release tension
    * Notice physical signs of control patterns
    * Use movement practices like yoga or tai chi

Shifting from Control to Flow

1. Develop adaptability:
    * Remain flexible when plans change
    * View obstacles as opportunities
    * Practice spontaneity in safe situations

2. Build trust:
    * Start with small acts of letting go
    * Document positive outcomes from surrender
    * Create support systems for uncertainty

Action Steps

1. Daily practices:
    * Morning intention setting without attachment
    * Evening reflection on control patterns
    * Regular breaks for present-moment awareness

2. Weekly review:
    * Note situations where control created stress
    * Identify areas for practising acceptance
    * Celebrate moments of successful surrender

Remember: The goal isn't to eliminate control but to develop a healthier relationship with uncertainty and change. Start small, be patient, and trust the process.

3
Alignment and Purpose

In the heart of the bustling city, a young woman named Sophia dashed through the crowded streets, her heels clicking rapidly on the pavement. With a crisp blazer, sleek laptop bag, and perpetually buzzing smartphone, she looked like the quintessential modern professional – polished, focused, and forever in a rush.

Sophia had achieved what many would consider the markers of success. At just 28, she was already a rising star at her corporate firm, with an impressive salary, a high-rise apartment, and a jam-packed social calendar. She put in long hours, networked relentlessly, and never said no to a request, driven by a fierce determination to climb the ladder.

Yet despite her outward achievements, Sophia harboured a painful secret: she was deeply unhappy.

Beneath her polished veneer, stress and anxiety were her constant companions. She frequently worked into the wee hours, fuelled by coffee and adrenaline, only to wake up exhausted and dreading another day. The projects she poured herself into felt soulless, and the praise from her bosses rang hollow. She had little time for the things that truly lit her up – painting, being in nature, and deep conversations with loved ones. Life had become an endless slog of tasks and obligations, with dwindling pockets of joy.

Sophia's story is all too common in our modern world. So many of us feel perpetually stressed and chronically unfulfilled, even as we achieve conventional success. We set goals, make plans, fill our calendars... but rarely pause to ask if all this activity is truly aligned with what matters most. In the words of Henry David Thoreau, "It is not enough to be busy; so are the ants. The question is: What are we busy about?"

The Disconnect Within

At the root of so much stress is a fundamental misalignment – a gap between our deepest values and the way we actually spend our time and energy. We live at odds with our true priorities, chasing after external markers of success while neglecting the inner dimensions that make life worth living.

This plays out in myriad arenas: The high-powered lawyer who secretly yearns to be a musician. The busy mom who pours herself into everyone else's needs while her own passions gather dust. The entrepreneur who grinds away at a startup while his health and relationships deteriorate. When we're out of sync with our core self, everything feels harder than it needs to be, like pedalling a bike with a rusty chain, requiring immense effort to go a short distance.

Psychologists call this "cognitive dissonance" – the mental stress and discomfort that arise when our actions don't align with our beliefs or values. The greater the gap, the greater the inner tension. We can numb this discomfort for a while through distractions and denial – workaholism, substance abuse, compulsive busyness. But eventually, the truth catches up to us through symptoms like burnout, depression, anxiety, and that unshakeable sense that something is missing.

The truth is, we can achieve every outward marker of success and still feel bereft if those achievements aren't an authentic expression of who we are. As author Neil Gaiman wisely said, "The one thing that you have that nobody else has is you. Your voice, your mind, your story, your vision. So write and draw and build and play and dance and live as only you can."

The Call of Dharma

So how do we close this gap and craft a life of deep integrity? The ancient yogic concept of Dharma offers a powerful roadmap. Dharma refers to our sacred duty – the unique expression of gifts and passions we're meant to offer in service of the world. When we're in alignment with our Dharma, we feel a profound sense of purpose, vitality, and flow. Stress melts into the background as we're carried forward by an inexplicable grace.

Finding our Dharma is a journey of radical self-honesty. It demands peeling back the layers of who we think we should be to uncover the truth of who we are. This requires introspection, experimentation, and the courage to march to the beat of our own drum. Rumi captured it beautifully: "Let yourself be silently drawn by the strange pull of what you really love. It will not lead you astray."

One way to begin is by clarifying our core values – the guiding principles that anchor and animate our lives. Values are different from goals in that they're ongoing qualities of being rather than measurable endpoints. Examples might include creativity, compassion, adventure, freedom, service, and excellence. When our lives and work are an authentic reflection of our values, we feel a sense of wholeness and ease.

Next, we can inventory our innate gifts – the unique amalgam of talents, passions, and quirks that make us perfectly suited for certain roles. This includes not just formal skills but those ineffable qualities that come so naturally we assume everyone has them. Perhaps it's an artistic flair, a compassionate ear, a visionary mind, or an infectious zest for life. When we harness these gifts in service of something larger, we become a conduit for inspired contribution.

From this foundation, we can begin aligning our lifestyle and work with our Dharma. This is a courageous act of restructuring – of saying no to what's no longer congruent and saying a full-bodied yes to our soul's calling. It means setting boundaries, having vulnerable conversations, and taking leaps into the unknown. At times, it may feel risky, even irresponsible. But as we taste the sweetness of authentic living, we realize nothing could be more responsible than embodying our truth.

Crafting a Life of Integrity

Of course, living our Dharma is not a one-time decision but an ongoing devotional practice. It's a commitment to staying true to ourselves amidst the onslaught of obligations, expectations, and shiny distractions. Which beckons the question: how can we set up our lives to support rather than hinder our soul's journey?

One key is building rhythms and routines that keep us anchored in our values. This means carving out inviolable time for the activities that fill our cup, whether that's morning meditation, daily walks in nature, a weekly artist's date, or regular adventures with loved ones. When we treat these practices as sacred, they infuse the rest of life with meaning and vitality.

It also helps to curate our environment to mirror our true priorities. Is our space cluttered with remnants of a past self, or does it reflect who we're becoming? Do the images and objects around us inspire expansiveness or constriction? As we attune our habitat to our essence, we create an outer topology that nurtures rather than depletes our energy.

Equally vital are the people we surround ourselves with. Jim Rohn said we become the average of the five people we spend the most time with. Who are the allies that see us in our fullness, that call forth our greatest self? Who are the teachers and mentors who stretch us towards our edge? When we cultivate a tribe of truth-tellers, we find ourselves lifted by the cadence of our collective Dharma.

Purpose as a Path

Perhaps the most profound shift happens when we reframe purpose not as a fixed destination but as a dynamic unfolding. So often we put immense pressure on ourselves to find our "one true calling", as if there's a singular cosmic plan we must discover and rigidly adhere to. But when we relax this notion, we start to see purpose as a fluid conversation with life – an improvisational dance in which we co-create the steps as we go.

From this perspective, authentic living is more about the qualities of presence, attunement, and responsiveness we bring to each moment than about the specific roles we inhabit. It's about showing up fully, listening deeply, and offering our unique gift as best we can. As the needs of the world shift, so too does the shape of our offering. Like a sunflower perpetually pivoting towards the light, we turn in the direction of our evolving edge.

This orientation requires immense trust in ourselves, in the intelligence of life, in the value of our innate being. It demands relinquishing the compulsion to contrive and control, and instead surrendering to the exquisite uncertainty of the journey. When the Sufi mystic Hazrat Inayat Khan was asked how he managed to compose such luminous music, he replied: "I do not compose. I simply remove the veil and let the music play itself."

In the same way, when we remove the veils of fear, judgement, and second-guessing, we give our Dharma permission to play itself through us. We step into a radical flow state where action becomes effortless, synchronicities abound, and our service merges with our bliss. Stress transmutes into an enlivening stretch – the sensation of pushing our edges in delightful devotion to our highest calling.

Walking Each Other Home

As we travel this path of purpose, it's crucial to remember we're not walking it alone. At a primordial level, our Dharma is always in dialogue with the greater Dharma of the whole. We're each vital threads in the resplendent tapestry of being, inextricably woven into the collective dream. How we show up ripples out, in seen and unseen ways, touching realms beyond our imagining.

In this way, aligning with our soul's path is not a solitary act but a sacred form of activism. When we embody authentic presence, we give others permission to do the same. When we honour our inner truth, we create space for radical honesty in our relationships. When we let our singular light shine, we puncture holes in the trance of separation and scarcity.

As author and teacher Ram Dass poignantly expressed, "We are all just walking each other home." No matter how else we earn our livelihood, this is our fundamental vocation – to help each other awaken to the luminous reality of our shared being. What could be more meaningful, more important, than that?

Dear reader, I invite you to join me in the practice of purposeful living. To commit, again and again, to listening past the clamour of expectation to the crystal clarity of your inner knowing. To restructure your life, as best you're able, to be a sanctuary for your soul's unfolding. To honour the sacred story that only you can tell, the singular gift that only you can give.

In those moments when you find yourself stressed and straining, when you feel the ache of misalignment, I invite you to pause and simply ask: "What wants to live through me now?" Then breathe deeply, drop into your heart, and wait for the whispered response. Trust what comes, however faint, however foreign. Let the intelligence of your Dharma guide you, one choice at a time, back to your truth and your tribe.

As you walk this path of embodied purpose, take heart in the knowledge that you are part of a great remembering. With each courageous step, you inch the human story forward, midwifing a world in which authenticity is the norm and love is the law. You are needed, so needed, exactly as you are. May you trust the perfection of your unfolding and embrace the rapture of being alive.

Alignment and Purpose – Practical Takeaways

Identifying Misalignment

1. Assess your current state:
   * Track energy levels throughout daily activities
   * Note which tasks drain vs. energize you
   * Identify recurring stress triggers
   * Record moments of flow and fulfilment

2. Evaluate key life areas:
   * Career alignment with core values
   * Quality of relationships
   * Time spent on priorities
   * Balance between obligations and passions

Discovering Your Dharma

1. Clarify core values:
   * List what matters most to you
   * Examine influences on your choices
   * Define non-negotiable principles
   * Review past peak experiences

2. Map your gifts:
   * Natural talents and abilities
   * Activities that energize you
   * Skills others frequently seek from you
   * Contributions that feel effortless

Creating Alignment

1. Restructure daily routines:
    * Schedule time for essential practices
    * Create boundaries around energy drains
    * Build in regular reflection periods
    * Prioritize activities that align with values

2. Adjust your environment:
    * Declutter spaces that create stress
    * Organize surroundings to support priorities
    * Curate inspiring visual elements
    * Create zones for different activities

Cultivating Support

1. Build your tribe:
    * Connect with aligned individuals
    * Seek mentors and guides
    * Join communities with shared values
    * Distance from depleting relationships

2. Establish accountability:
    * Share your intentions with trusted allies
    * Regular check-ins on alignment goals
    * Document progress and insights
    * Celebrate small wins and shifts

Action Steps

1. Daily practices:
   * Morning intention setting
   * Mindful transitions between activities
   * Evening reflection on alignment
   * Gratitude for authentic moments

2. Weekly review:
   * Assess alignment in key areas
   * Adjust plans based on energy levels
   * Plan meaningful activities
   * Release what no longer serves

3. Monthly reset:
   * Review broader life direction
   * Update goals and priorities
   * Evaluate relationships and commitments
   * Plan next steps for greater alignment

Remember: Alignment is an ongoing process, not a destination. Small, consistent adjustments create lasting change.

4
Mind Matters

In a dimly lit room, a man sat hunched over his desk, his face illuminated by the harsh glow of the computer screen. Marcus had been staring at the same spreadsheet for hours, his mind racing with worst-case scenarios. The project deadline was looming, his team was behind schedule, and his boss had hinted at budget cuts. As he clicked frantically through the data, a familiar chorus of thoughts looped through his head: "You're going to fail. You're not cut out for this. Everyone will see you're a fraud."

Marcus felt his chest tighten and his breath grow shallow. A knot of dread settled in his stomach as the thoughts grew increasingly catastrophic. By the time he finally shut off his computer and crawled into bed, his mind was a battlefield of anxiety and self-doubt. He tossed and turned for hours, desperately trying to silence the inner critic that haunted him.

Marcus's story is a familiar one in our stress-laden world. No matter how outwardly successful or put-together we may appear, most of us are engaged in a secret war with our own minds. Incessant worry, self-judgement, regret about the past, anxiety about the future – this mental chatter is so ubiquitous we often assume it's just the price of being human.

But what if it didn't have to be this way? What if stress were not an inevitable part of life but a byproduct of our unexamined thoughts? What if we could relate to our inner world in a radically different way – one that allowed us to face challenges with clarity, resilience, and even playfulness?

The truth is, the quality of our mind directly shapes the quality of our life. Beneath every stressful experience lies a stressful thought – an interpretation or assumption we've taken to be reality. When we believe our thoughts unquestioningly, we get swept into a virtual reality of suffering, losing sight of the innate peace that's possible in the present moment. But when we learn to notice and question our thoughts, we discover immense freedom to live and respond in new ways.

The Landscape of Mind

To understand the crucial link between stress and thinking, it helps to explore the terrain of the mind. Far from a unified entity, the mind is more like an orchestra of different voices, each with its own agenda and intent. There's the rational mind that figures and plans, the emotional mind that feels and reacts, the primitive mind obsessed with survival. In any given moment, these different aspects are all piping up, often with conflicting messages.

The loudest (and often most stressed) voice tends to be that of the ego – the mind's sense of separate self. The ego's job is to construct and maintain a coherent identity, to make meaning of our experience in a way that preserves our self-image. It will go to great lengths to feel in control, interpreting events through the lens of "what does this mean about me?"

This is a useful function, allowing us to learn from experience and navigate a complex world. But when the ego runs the show unexamined, it creates immense stress. Constantly defending and promoting itself, the ego filters reality through a distorted lens of fear – fear of failure, rejection, loss, and death. It compulsively rehashes the past and rehearses the future, keeping us trapped in imagined storylines cut off from the aliveness of the present.

The ego is also the birthplace of the inner critic, that relentless fault-finder that picks apart our every move. Desperate to feel worthy and sufficient, the critic constantly compares us to unrealistic ideals, shaming us when we fall short. It's the voice that sneers "You're not good enough" or "Who do you think you are?", eroding our sense of innate worth.

Identifying with this ego-mind leads to tremendous suffering. Instead of meeting life with fresh eyes, we get lost in a virtual reality of judgement and reactivity. We feel perpetually on edge, disconnected from our deeper wisdom and suffocated by chronic stress. As the great sage Ramana Maharshi put it, "The mind is a bundle of thoughts. The thoughts arise because there is a thinker. The thinker is the ego. The ego, if sought, will automatically vanish."

The Power of Awareness

So, how do we loosen the tyrannical grip of the ego-mind and reclaim our natural ease? The first step is to recognize that we are not our thoughts – we are the awareness behind them. No matter how compelling they may seem, our thoughts are simply fleeting phenomena passing through the vast field of our consciousness. We don't have to believe them or get sucked into their drama.

With this recognition comes immense freedom.

Instead of fusing with our mental chatter, we can start to observe it with curiosity and compassion. We become like the sky, watching the clouds drift by – vast, open, and unperturbed by the passing weather. This witnessing awareness is our true home, the timeless backdrop against which all experience arises and dissolves.

One powerful way to cultivate this awareness is through mindfulness meditation. By anchoring our attention in the present moment – on the breath, the body, or the senses – we learn to disentangle from the mind stream and rest in our essential beingness. Each time we notice a thought and gently escort our attention back to the Now, we strengthen our capacity to meet life free from the filter of ego.

Another potent practice is self-inquiry, or investigating the nature of the mind directly. By turning towards our thoughts with genuine interest and questioning their validity, we start to see through their illusion of solidity. We might ask: "Is this really true? How do I know? What if the opposite were true?" As we shine the light of awareness on our patterns of reactivity, they gradually lose their power to control us.

These practices aren't about suppressing or eliminating thoughts – that would only create more tension and stress. Rather, they're an invitation to change our relationship to thinking, to discover the spacious awareness that's always available beneath the turbulence of the mind. In the words of Eckhart Tolle: "The primary cause of unhappiness is never the situation but your thoughts about it."

Belief Systems and Stress

Beyond the moment-to-moment chatter of the mind, our stress is also deeply shaped by our underlying belief systems. Beliefs are the lenses through which we filter reality, the implicit assumptions that colour our perception and drive our behaviour. While some beliefs are conscious and articulable, many operate beneath the surface, quietly shaping our lives without our awareness.

These belief systems are formed through a complex interplay of factors – our upbringing, cultural conditioning, pivotal experiences, and the coping mechanisms we've learned along the way. They span all domains of life, from our worthiness and lovability to the nature of success and failure to our basic trust in existence. When unexamined, limiting beliefs create a tremendous amount of stress and suffering.

Take Marcus, for instance. Beneath his anxiety about the project lies a deep-seated belief that his worth is contingent on his performance – that he has to constantly prove himself to be acceptable. This likely stems from early experiences of conditional love, where affection and approval were doled out based on achievement. Overlaid on this is a belief that failure is catastrophic, a sign of inherent deficiency rather than a natural part of growth.

These hidden beliefs create a hothouse of pressure and perfectionism, where Marcus feels perpetually on trial, terrified of being exposed as a fraud. He pushes himself relentlessly, unable to rest or celebrate his successes, always raising the bar to unattainable heights. It's a recipe for burnout, a joyless striving that leaves him disconnected from his deeper self.

Making the Unconscious Conscious

To uproot limiting beliefs, we must first bring them into the light of consciousness. This requires turning towards our stress with open and compassionate attention, getting curious about the hidden assumptions driving our experience. We might ask: "What must I believe in order to feel this way? What core beliefs are being activated here?"

As we investigate our patterns with patience and care, the unconscious becomes conscious – we start to see the learned beliefs shaping our reality. This in itself is liberating, as it allows us to question their validity and consider new possibilities. We can hold our beliefs lightly, as working hypotheses rather than statements of fact, and update them as we grow and evolve.

It's important to approach this process with immense self-compassion, recognizing that our beliefs are not our fault – they're survival strategies we learned to navigate an imperfect world. Blaming or shaming ourselves only compounds the stress and keeps us stuck in old patterns. Instead, we can meet ourselves with kindness and understanding, appreciating the innocent intentions beneath even our most neurotic tendencies.

As we expose and release limiting beliefs, we create space for a more authentic and empowering worldview to emerge. We can consciously choose beliefs that align with our deepest truths and values, that support our growth and well-being. This is an ongoing practice of self-creation, of becoming the author of our own reality.

The Stories We Live By

At the deepest level, our stress is a function of the stories we tell – about ourselves, others, and the world at large. The human mind is a meaning-making machine, weaving disparate bits of perception into elaborate narratives. These narratives shape our identity, defining who we are and how life happens to us.

All too often, our stories are rooted in lack and separation – we cast ourselves as isolated beings in a hostile world, doomed to perpetual struggle. The "I'm not enough" story, the "Life is hard" story, the "I'm all alone" story – these well-worn grooves keep us trapped in suffering, unable to see the wholeness and beauty that's always available.

But what if we could rewrite these stories? What if we could consciously author a new narrative, one that aligned with our highest truth and deepest joy? This is the transformative power of storytelling – by changing the lens through which we view reality, we change reality itself.

One potent practice is to examine our stories through the lens of a loving and wise mentor. Imagine you could travel through time and offer counsel to your younger self. What stories would you gently question or update? What larger perspectives would you offer? How might you invite that tender self into a more integrated and empowered narrative?

Another powerful inquiry is to ask: "What would the story be if it were written in utter love?" How would we make sense of our challenges and traumas if we held them in a context of unconditional compassion? What hidden gifts and lessons might we find woven through even our most difficult chapters?

As we consciously craft a more expansive story, we open to profound possibilities for healing and growth. We start to see challenges as invitations to evolve, relationships as mirrors of our own wholeness, and life itself as a great adventure of the soul. Stress melts into the background as we realize our inherent okayness, our unbreakable belonging to the web of creation.

The Ultimate Medicine

Ultimately, the greatest balm for a stressed mind is the recognition of our essential nature as conscious presence. Beneath the turmoil of thoughts and stories lies a vast stillness that's eternally at peace. This is our true self – the timeless awareness in which all experience arises and dissolves like ripples on the ocean.

Tapping into this inner dimension is the ultimate medicine, for it reconnects us with our inherent wholeness and completion. When rooted in presence, we can meet the fluctuations of life with unshakeable resilience. Difficulties still arise, but we're no longer fused with them – we can navigate challenges with spaciousness and grace.

To access this wellspring of peace, we need not wait for the mind to settle or circumstances to change. The gateway is always available in the power of the present moment. By bringing our full attention to the here and now – the felt experience of the breath, the body, the senses – we ground ourselves in the living reality beyond thought.

This is a radical act in our chronically distracted world. It's an invitation to shift from doing to being, from mental time travel to embodied presence. As we learn to disentangle from the mind stream and rest in our essential nature, we taste true freedom – the freedom to meet life as it is and dance with the unfolding mystery.

Dear friend, I invite you to embrace this pathless path of presence. In this very breath, sense the alert stillness behind the mind – the boundless awareness that's always here. Feel into the aliveness of your body, the vibrancy coursing through every cell. Open your senses to the wild beauty of the world, the shimmering miracle of the ordinary.

As you navigate the inevitable stresses of life, remember that peace is your birthright. It's not something to be chased on the horizon but something to be uncovered within. Your natural state is one of ease and lightness, no matter what the mind may tell you. No thought or story can ever diminish the radiance of your being.

So come home to yourself, again and again. Question the beliefs that keep you trapped in lack and learn to tell a more winsome story. Whenever you find yourself hooked, celebrate this moment of remembering and gently return to the Now. Breathe, soften, allow – and let the effortless grace of your true nature carry you home.

May your journey be blessed with laughter, insight, and the joyful realization of your unassailable wholeness. May you come to see all experience as an invitation to awaken, to fully embrace this wild and precious life. And may you know, beyond doubt, the profound peace that surpasses understanding.

Mind Matters – Practical Takeaways

Understanding Your Mind

1. Map your mental landscape:
   * Track thought patterns throughout the day
   * Notice recurring themes and triggers
   * Identify your common stress narratives
   * Observe your inner critic's voice

2. Recognize thought distortions:
   * Catastrophizing (assuming worst outcomes)
   * Black-and-white thinking
   * Mind reading (assuming others' thoughts)
   * Over-personalizing events

Mindfulness Practices

1. Daily meditation:
   * Start with 5-10 minutes of breath awareness
   * Notice thoughts without engaging them
   * Return attention gently when distracted
   * Gradually increase duration

2. Present moment anchors:
   * Use physical sensations as reminders
   * Practice mindful transitions
   * Engage fully with simple tasks
   * Connect with body sensations regularly

Transforming Beliefs

1. Examine core beliefs:
   * List your assumptions about success/failure
   * Question inherited family beliefs
   * Notice beliefs about self-worth
   * Identify limiting patterns

2. Update belief systems:
   * Challenge negative assumptions
   * Gather evidence that contradicts limitations
   * Create new empowering beliefs
   * Test beliefs through small experiments

Rewriting Your Story

1. Assess current narratives:
   * Write your dominant life stories
   * Identify recurring themes
   * Notice victim/hero patterns
   * Examine the story's impact on stress

2. Create new narratives:
    * Reframe challenges as growth
    * Include multiple perspectives
    * Acknowledge personal agency
    * Integrate wisdom gained

Action Steps

1. Daily practices:
    * Morning thought awareness
    * Midday belief check-ins
    * Evening story reflection
    * Regular meditation sessions

2. Weekly review:
    * Journal about mental patterns
    * Update limiting beliefs
    * Celebrate mindfulness progress
    * Plan next week's practice focus

Remember: Transforming your mind is a gradual process. Start small, be consistent, and approach the journey with self-compassion.

5
Connection and Support

Jana wiped away the tears streaming down her face as she sat alone in her parked car. The argument with her partner played over and over in her mind, his harsh words stinging like salt in a wound. This was just the latest blow in a season of struggle – ever since losing her job, Jana had felt like she was drowning, barely keeping her head above water. The stress was eating away at her, body and soul, but she couldn't see a way out.

As she scrolled numbly through her phone, Jana paused on the name of an old friend – someone she hadn't talked to in years. Part of her longed to reach out, to pour out her heart and be seen in her pain. But another voice stopped her – the voice that whispered she was a burden, that her struggles were hers alone to bear. "I don't want to bother anyone," Jana thought wearily. "They have their own problems to deal with."

Wiping her eyes, she tossed the phone aside and turned the key in the ignition, preparing to drive home to an empty apartment. As the engine hummed to life, Jana felt a wave of loneliness crash over her – a soul-deep ache for comfort and connection she dared not acknowledge.

Jana's story echoes the silent suffering of countless individuals in our modern world. In an age of hyper-connectivity, we find ourselves increasingly cut off from the nourishing bonds of community and support. Hiding behind curated social media feeds and the veneer of self-sufficiency, we navigate life's trials and stresses alone, convinced that our struggles make us weak or unlovable.

But this isolation comes at a steep cost. Volumes of research confirm what the heart intuitively knows: Connection is crucial for our well-being. It's the invisible matrix through which resilience, healing, and joy flow. When we belong to a web of supportive relationships – whether familial, platonic, or romantic – we're better able to weather the storms of life with grace and grit.

On the flip side, loneliness and isolation are toxic to the body, mind, and spirit. Studies link chronic loneliness to a higher risk of heart disease, dementia, depression, anxiety, and premature death. It wreaks havoc on our nervous systems, locking us in states of perpetual fight-flight-freeze. Cut off from the regulating presence of others, we're more prone to stress, reactivity, and illness on every level.

The Primal Need to Belong

To understand the vital role of connection, we must appreciate the evolutionary roots of our social wiring. For the vast majority of our history, human beings lived in close-knit tribes characterized by strong kinship bonds and shared responsibility for survival. Belonging to the group wasn't optional – it was a primal necessity in a world filled with predators and perils at every turn.

In this ancestral context, social rejection or ostracism amounted to a death sentence. Without the protection and provisions of the tribe, an individual's chance of survival plummeted. As a result, our brains developed sophisticated circuitry to monitor our social standing and raise the alarm at any hint of exclusion. The pain of isolation is processed in the same neural networks as physical pain – a compelling incentive to preserve our place in the group.

While the threats have changed, this hardwiring remains intact. In a very real sense, we're still walking around in Stone Age bodies, navigating a world of iPhones and jet travel with brains optimized for the savanna. Our nervous systems constantly scan for cues of acceptance or rejection, safety or danger in our connections with others. When we feel securely bonded, our stress-response system stays in a resting state, allowing us to relax, regenerate, and explore. But when we sense disconnection or exclusion, alarm bells start ringing – flooding us with anxiety, shame, and a primal fear for survival.

The Myth of Self-Sufficiency

Despite this innate need for belonging, we live in a culture that exalts self-sufficiency as the highest virtue. From a young age, we're steeped in messages that valorize independence, grit, and going it alone. Vulnerability is viewed as weakness, neediness as pathology. We're told that maturity means outgrowing our basic human need for love, comfort, and support.

This myth is perpetuated in our heroic archetypes, our bootstrap narratives of success, even our definitions of adulthood itself. The rugged individual, the self-made man, the solo adventurer – these figures loom large in our collective imagination, shaping our assumptions about what it means to be strong, capable, and worthy.

But this ideal is profoundly misguided and psychologically destructive. As the poet John Donne famously wrote, "No man is an island." We're intrinsically interdependent creatures, wired for connection at every level. Our very sense of self emerges through the mirroring presence of others – we come to know ourselves through the reflection of their care and attunement.

When we buy into the myth of self-sufficiency, we sever ourselves from this fundamental matrix of belonging. We exile ourselves to a desert of isolation, convinced that our worthiness depends on going it alone. We strive, achieve, and accumulate – all in a desperate attempt to prove our enoughness. But no amount of external success can fill the aching void within.

This inner disconnect breeds immense stress and suffering. When we're cut off from the regulating presence of others, we're far more vulnerable to anxiety, depression, addiction, and disease. Our nervous systems get stuck in chronic fight-flight-freeze, unable to return to baseline. We feel perpetually on edge, armoured against life and numb to our own hearts.

The Power of Presence

The antidote to this epidemic of disconnection is disarmingly simple: authentic, attuned presence. It's the felt sense of being seen, heard, and held in our totality – not just our polished facade but our tender, messy humanity. In the company of a caring other, we remember the safety and sufficiency that's our birthright. We come home to the nourishing ground of our being.

This kind of presence is a rare gift in our fast-paced,

distracted world. So often, we move through life only half-available – one eye on our screens, one foot out the door, minds churning with elsewhere plans. We listen to respond rather than to understand, more focused on fixing or advising than on fully taking in another's experience. Uncomfortable with the rawness of real intimacy, we hide behind masks and manoeuvres, keeping our exchanges safe and superficial.

But true connection requires vulnerability, the willingness to show up and be seen in our tender truth. It asks us to put down our phones, agendas and armour – to arrive with open hearts and curious minds. To listen beneath the words to the feelings and needs expressed. To offer our full-bodied attention as a sacred space in which others can unfold.

This quality of presence is deeply regulating our nervous systems. When we feel met in our essence – not judged, shamed or fixed but simply held with care – our bodies instinctively relax. The hypervigilance of the stress response gives way to the nourishing peace of the parasympathetic state. Digestion, immune function, and cellular repair all come online as we rest in the safety of the bond.

Moreover, attuned connection literally rewires our brains for resilience and well-being. Through the vehicle of secure attachment, we internalize a sense of safety, belongingness, and worthiness. We develop the capacity to soothe ourselves in times of distress and reach out for support when needed. Our window of tolerance for life's ups and downs expands, allowing us to meet challenges with flexibility and grace.

Cultivating Caring Community

So, how do we create more of these nourishing connections in our lives and world? It starts with prioritizing relationships as the foundation of a meaningful life. In a culture obsessed with achievement and acquisition, it's easy to relegate our bonds to the back burner – to view them as nice-to-haves rather than must-haves for our well-being. But when we put people first – when we invest time and energy into cultivating caring community – we weave a web of resilience that carries us through life's storms.

One powerful practice is to conduct a life audit through the lens of connection. Review how you spend your time and energy in a typical week. What percentage goes towards nourishing your relationships – with family, friends, community, and your own tender self? What gets de-prioritized in the addictive busy-ness of modern life? Identify small steps you could take to carve out more space for the people and pursuits that truly feed your soul.

Another key is learning to reach out and ask for support, especially in times of struggle. So many of us have internalized the belief that our pain is a private burden, that needing help means we're broken or deficient. But the truth is, we all need extra holding at times – it's part of the human inheritance. Daring to make the call, send the text, or voice the vulnerable request is a radical act of self-love and empowered interdependence.

It's equally vital to normalize struggle and embrace the shadow both in ourselves and others. So often, the sheen of social media perpetuates an illusion of perfectionism, a highlight reel in which everyone else seems to have it all together. This breeds immense shame and isolation when we find ourselves in the inevitable muck of being human. What if we dared to share the full truth of our experience – not in a spirit of victimhood but vulnerable authenticity? What if we created spaces where the real mess of the heart was welcomed and held?

Attuning to Essence

Beyond specific relationships, we can cultivate a baseline of connection through the quality of presence we bring to life itself. When rooted in essence, we realize our intrinsic belongingness to the web of being – the indivisible wholeness that's the true nature of reality. We see that separation is a perceptual illusion, a trick of the conceptual mind. On the deepest level, there's no gap between self and other, human and nature, creature and cosmos. We're each shimmering expressions of a singular aliveness, ripples in a seamless ocean of being.

Tapping into this ground of connection is the ultimate medicine for the stressed and lonely soul. When we attune to the living miracle of the present moment – the vastness of the sky, the solidity of the earth, the pulse of our own heartbeat – we plug into a wellspring of nourishment that's always available. We remember the indigenous belonging that's our deepest birthright.

This remembrance doesn't negate the importance of human bonds, but rather contextualizes them in a larger field of connection. We're liberated from the myth of the separate self, the painful trance of isolation. We recognize each being, from our most cherished beloveds to the stranger on the street, as a unique radiance of the same essential light. Our hearts break open with the beauty and pathos of this shared predicament, this precious chance to participate in the unfolding story of life.

In the crucible of presence, our wounds and armour soften, revealing the tenderness at our core. We find the courage to show up fully – to love without holding back, to risk the terrible vulnerability of an open heart. We learn to lean into the discomfort of authentic intimacy, trusting that connection is our deepest nature and truest home. And we discover that the key to navigating life's stresses with resilience is not self-sufficiency but profound interdependence – the humble recognition of how much we all need each other.

A Call to Connection

Dear friend, I invite you into the revolutionary act of prioritizing presence – in your relationship with others, the living world, and your own tender heart. Dare to put people and passion first, to carve out time for what truly feeds your soul. Risk reaching out and letting yourself be seen in the raw truth of your humanity. And have compassion for the parts that resist vulnerability, that still cling to the myth of the separate self.

As you walk this path, be patient and kind with your inevitable stumbles. The journey from armoured isolation to openhearted connection is a long and winding road. Honour the protector parts that once kept you safe, the only way they knew how. At the same time, practice relaxing your guard and resting in your innate enoughness. Little by little, learn to receive love and support as your divine birthright.

When the stress and struggle surface, as they surely will, reach out and let yourself be held. Have the courage to ask for what you need, to voice the scary or shameful secret. And when you find yourself in the role of listener, offer your full-hearted presence as the rarest of medicines. Put down the phone, the inner commentary, the compulsion to fix – and simply bear witness to what's alive. Let your caring attention be a sanctuary in which others can come home to themselves.

Above all, remember: You belong. Your being is a needed part of the endless symphonic expression of life. The universe longs for your unique note, the flavour of reality only you can sing. There's unspeakable beauty in the singular radiance that you are – the unrepeatable wonderment of each moment's blossoming. How astonishing and precious it is to be here at all!

So let us practice the art of connection, in all its gritty glory. Let us weave a web of resilience, one moment of presence at a time. Let us dare to love in a world that's forgotten how to surrender our defences and come home to the safety of the heart. And let us anchor ourselves in the indigenous belonging that's always been here, holding us in its sheltering embrace.

May you know yourself as intimately woven into the miracle of life, a sacred cell in the dreaming body of the cosmos. May you find solace and strength in the kinship of your fellow travellers, the billions of beings walking each other home. And may you rest in the luminous awareness that you are never, ever alone – held always in the infinite heart of love.

Connection and Support – Practical Takeaways

Assessing Your Connection Landscape

1. Audit your relationships:
   * Map close connections vs. acquaintances
   * Identify supportive vs. draining relationships
   * Note areas needing more connection
   * Evaluate digital vs. in-person interaction balance

2. Review time allocation:
   * Track relationship investment
   * Note missed connection opportunities
   * Identify connection barriers
   * Plan dedicated connection time

Building Authentic Connections

1. Practice deep listening:
   * Remove distractions during conversations
   * Focus on understanding vs. responding
   * Notice non-verbal cues
   * Ask clarifying questions

2. Cultivate vulnerability:
   * Share genuine feelings
   * Express needs clearly
   * Ask for support when needed
   * Acknowledge struggles openly

Strengthening Support Systems

1. Create connection rituals:
    * Schedule regular check-ins
    * Plan shared activities
    * Create group traditions
    * Establish support circles

2. Develop community:
    * Join interest-based groups
    * Participate in local events
    * Volunteer for causes
    * Create gathering spaces

Nurturing Presence

1. Daily connection practices:
    * Morning check-ins with loved ones
    * Mindful meals together
    * Technology-free quality time
    * Bedtime connection rituals

2. Self-connection practices:
    * Regular self-reflection time
    * Nature connection periods
    * Body awareness exercises
    * Creative expression

Action Steps

1. Weekly practices:
    * Reach out to one person
    * Have one deep conversation
    * Practice vulnerability
    * Engage in group activities

2. Monthly review:
    * Evaluate connection quality
    * Update support network
    * Plan community engagement
    * Adjust connection strategies

Remember: Building authentic connections takes time and courage. Start with small steps and gradually expand your support network.

6
Balancing Being and Doing

Liam sat at his desk, staring blankly at the endless to-do list glaring back at him from the computer screen. It was only 10 am, but he already felt behind, his mind churning with all the tasks and obligations stretched out before him. The more he tried to focus, the more his attention scattered, jumping from project to project, worry to worry, never fully landing on anything.

As the day wore on, Liam's body grew increasingly tense, his breath shallow and constricted. By evening, he felt like a wrung-out dishrag – exhausted but strangely wired, his nervous system buzzing with a frenetic energy he couldn't seem to shake. Even as he fell into bed, his mind continued to race – replaying the day's stresses, rehearsing tomorrow's challenges, a hamster wheel of rumination that made deep rest an elusive dream.

Liam's experience is all too common in our modern world of relentless doing. Swept up in a culture that glorifies busyness and productivity, we move through our days in a state of perpetual motion – rushing from one task to the next, forever trying to cross items off an ever-growing to-do list. Even our leisure time has become scheduled and optimized, just another item to check off in the pursuit of self-improvement.

The costs of this chronic overdrive are steep. When we're constantly doing, we lose touch with the nourishing rhythm of being – the spacious, embodied presence that's our deepest nature. Cut off from this wellspring of vitality, we become increasingly stressed, anxious, and depleted. Our sympathetic nervous systems get stuck in the "on" position, flooding our bodies with stress hormones that wreak havoc over time. We feel alienated from ourselves, each other, and the living world – hungry ghosts grasping for fulfilment in all the wrong places.

At the heart of this imbalance is a fundamental misunderstanding of the nature of time. Trapped on the hamster wheel of doing, we relate to time as a linear commodity – a scarce resource that we must endlessly race against. The future is seen as something "out there", a destination to be rushed towards with grit and sweat. The present becomes a means to an end, a stepping stone to be hurried over in the quest for later gratification.

But in the words of spiritual teacher Eckhart Tolle, "Time isn't precious at all, because it is an illusion. What you perceive as precious is not time but the one point that is out of time: the Now. That is precious indeed. The more you are focused on time — past and future-the more you miss the Now, the most precious thing there is."

The Timeless Now

When we drop out of the mind's obsession with past and future, we discover the nourishing ground of presence that's always available, right here and now. We touch into a dimension beyond the constructs of linear time – the eternal Now that mystics and sages have pointed to throughout the ages. In this spacious stillness, we come home to our essential being – the boundless awareness in which all thoughts, feelings, and sensations arise and dissolve like waves on the ocean.

his quality of presence is our birthright, the natural state of the relaxed nervous system. When we're rooted in the Now, we feel deeply connected to life itself, attuned to the intelligence that animates every moment. Our senses come alive, revealing the extraordinary in the ordinary. We move through the world with a sense of ease, flow, and wonderment - marvelling at the miracle of existence.

Physiologically, tapping into presence activates the parasympathetic branch of the autonomic nervous system – the rest-and-digest response that calms the body and clears the mind. Stress hormones like cortisol and adrenaline decrease while feel-good neurotransmitters like serotonin and oxytocin increase. Digestion, immune function, and cellular repair all come online as we drop into a state of nourishing receptivity.

On a psychological level, being mode liberates us from the narrow confines of the ego – the mind-made self that's always chasing after fulfilment in some imagined future. We taste the peace that surpasses understanding, the deep okay-ness that's independent of circumstances. Life ceases to be a problem to be solved and becomes an adventure to be savoured, one moment at a time.

Of course, this isn't to say that doing is bad or unnecessary. As human beings, we're intrinsically creative creatures – wired to make, explore, and express. The world turns on our capacity to set goals, solve problems, and translate visions into reality. Meaningful doing is part of what gives life purpose and direction.

The key is to root our doing in the fertile soil of being, to infuse our actions with the nourishing elixir of presence. When we act from this connected place, our doing takes on a different quality – one of effortlessness, synchronicity, and inspired flow. We move with the current of life rather than against it, trusting the intelligence of the moment to guide our steps.

Practices for Presence

So, how do we cultivate this quality of embodied presence in a world addicted to doing? It starts with intention – a commitment to prioritizing the timeless Now over the tyranny of clock time. By dedicating ourselves to presence as a daily practice, we gradually strengthen the neural pathways of mindful awareness, coming home to our senses again and again.

One foundational practice is meditation – the art of bringing kind attention to our moment-to-moment experience. Whether sitting on a cushion or walking in nature, we train ourselves to notice the mind's compulsive narratives without getting hooked by them. Over time, we discover the spacious awareness that's always here beneath the mental chatter – the sky-like consciousness in which thoughts and feelings arise and dissolve.

Another key practice is mindful movement – engaging in activities that sync the body and mind in the present moment. Yoga, tai chi, qigong, and conscious dance all cultivate the felt sense of aliveness that's the hallmark of presence. As we attune to the breath and the body's sensations, we come out of our heads and into the vividness of the Now.

Nature immersion is also a potent portal to presence. When we spend time in wild places – away from the distractions of technology and to-do lists – we remember our primal belongingness to the living earth. The patient rhythms of the natural world – the undulating waves, the swaying trees, the drifting clouds – all beckon us back to the timeless Now. In nature, it's easier to drop the myth of separation and rest in the interconnected web of being.

Relational practices are another key ingredient of a presence-centred life. When we bring our full attention to our interactions – listening deeply, speaking authentically, attuning to the energy between us – we create sacred space for real connection to happen. In the crucible of caring presence, our nervous systems sync up and our hearts open, revealing the shared vulnerability and strength of our human condition. We remember that we're all in this together, walking each other home.

Ultimately, the most powerful practice is simply to bring mindful awareness to whatever we're doing, moment by moment. Whether washing dishes, driving to work, or writing an email, we train ourselves to engage with full-bodied attention, sensing the aliveness that's always here when we show up for it. The Vietnamese Zen teacher Thich Nhat Hanh calls this "washing the dishes to wash the dishes" – letting the doing be its own reward, without rushing towards some imagined future completion.

As we practice presence in these ways, a profound shift starts to happen. The boundary between being and doing begins to dissolve, revealing the seamless flow of life in all its full-spectrum wholeness. We discover that it's possible to rest in open, spacious awareness while still engaging in meaningful activity – to be fully here while getting stuff done. The doing arises naturally from the fullness of being, like a wave rising up from the depths of the ocean.

From this integrated place, we can dance with the currents of life as they flow through us – riding the waves of inspiration, navigating challenges with grace, letting our unique genius shine through. Our actions become infused with a quality of effortless effort, relaxed precision, and divinely inspired play. The Taoist sage Chuang Tzu called this "the art of effortless action from being" – the supreme skill of aligning ourselves so completely with the Tao that our doing becomes an overflow of our deepest nature.

Embracing Sacred Rhythm

As we come into this balance of being and doing, we start to honour the organic rhythms of life – the sacred oscillation of effort and ease, the yin and yang pulsing through every cell of creation. We recognize that stress arises when we get out of sync with these natural cycles, pushing where we're called to pause, achieving where we're invited to allow.

Think of the seasons – the way that nature moves through predictable but ever-fresh phases of growth and regeneration. Spring is a time of visioning and planting seeds, summer of vigorous growth, autumn of harvest and completion, winter of incubation and renewal. When we live in harmony with these eternal rhythms, we ride the effortless grace at the heart of being. But when we resist them – when we cling to ceaseless productivity or refuse needed rest – stress and burnout are the inevitable result.

The same is true of the rhythms of day and night, work and play, inhale and exhale. Each phase has its own innate intelligence, its own gifts and challenges. By learning to surf these rhythmic waves – and to surrender into the stillpoints between them – we find the place of power and poise at the centre of the storm. We become the eye of the hurricane, the unruffled awareness that can hold it all with endless compassion.

What this looks like in practice will vary for each of us based on our unique constitution and life circumstances. But some common elements include:

- Bookending the day with periods of stillness and intentional being – whether a morning meditation, an evening gratitude practice, or simply some mindful breaths as we transition between activities.
- Honouring the body's need for rest and renewal – with regular breaks, restorative practices, and

sufficient sleep. Learning to listen to our organism's subtle signals and respond with loving care.

- Carving out regular time for play, creativity, and unstructured delight – pursuing activities that light us up from the inside out. Letting our inner child come out to frolic in the fields of life.
- Building a healthy relationship with technology – using it to serve rather than enslave us. Creating sacred tech-free zones and practising digital minimalism as an act of self-love.
- Aligning our schedules with our natural rhythms whenever possible – honouring our unique chronobiology and energy patterns. Working with rather than against the tides of our being.
- Cultivating an attitude of reverence for the preciousness of life – savouring sensory pleasures, celebrating small moments, marvelling at the miracle of the ordinary. Greet the gift of each moment with wonder and awe.

When we live in this way – dancing between doing and being, effort and surrender, expansion and contraction – we start to experience an unshakeable resilience in the face of life's stresses. Rooted in the infinite ground of Now, we're no longer thrown off centre by the inevitable ups and downs of existence. We navigate challenges with grace and grit, staying true to our deepest values in the midst of changing circumstances.

An Invitation to the Dance

Dear friend, I invite you to embrace this dance of sacred balance – to honour the cycles of your being while still engaging in purposeful doing. Start by bringing mindful presence to your daily activities, fully inhabiting the eternal Now available in each moment. Practice pausing throughout the day to connect with your breath and your body, attuning to the subtle signals of your inner landscape.

Notice when you're getting caught up in frenetic doing and gently bring yourself back to the nourishing ground of being. Remember that you are a human being, not a human doing. Your worth is not measured by your productivity but by your presence – the unique vibration that only you can offer in each moment.

At the same time, let your doing be an overflow of your deepest being – a joyful outpouring of your gifts and genius in service of something larger than yourself. Trust the intelligence of life to guide your actions, listening for the invitations and openings that are yours to dance with. Let your work become your worship, your art, your lovemaking – a sacred occasion to bring your whole self to the altar of life.

As you navigate this path, be gentle and patient with yourself. The balance of being and doing is not a destination but an ongoing practice, a continual coming home to the present moment. Honour the seasons of your soul, the organic wisdom of your body, the ineffable guidance of your heart. And when you stumble or stray, simply begin again – with a generous dose of self-compassion and a healthy sense of humour.

Above all, remember that you are part of a greater wholeness, a cosmic dance that's been going on long before you arrived and will continue long after you're gone. This is the dance of life itself – the eternal play of consciousness, the boundless creativity of the universe in motion. How blessed we are to be part of this grand unfolding, to lend our unique essence to the miracle of existence!

So let us embrace the fullness of this human adventure, with all its messy glory and heartbreaking beauty. Let us dance between doing and being, effort and ease, the timeless and the timely. Let us remember, again and again, the precious gift of presence – the eternal spring at the heart of all that is. And let us walk each other home to the vast, radiant Now, one mindful step at a time.

Balancing Being and Doing – Practical Takeaways

Assessing Balance

1. Audit your time:
    * Track doing vs. being activities
    * Note energy levels throughout the day
    * Identify peak productivity periods
    * Monitor stress triggers

2. Check rhythms:
    * Natural sleep-wake cycle
    * Energy fluctuations
    * Creative flow periods
    * Rest needs

Cultivating Presence

1. Daily mindfulness:
    * Morning meditation
    * Mindful transitions
    * Tech-free periods
    * Evening reflection

2. Body awareness:
    * Regular movement breaks
    * Breath check-ins
    * Body scanning
    * Nature connection time

Optimizing Action

1. Work practices:
    * Single-tasking focus periods
    * Strategic breaks
    * Priority alignment
    * Energy management

2. Task organization:
    * Essential vs. optional tasks
    * Energy-based scheduling
    * Buffer time between activities
    * Regular review periods

Creating Sacred Rhythm

1. Daily structure:
    * Morning sacred time
    * Mindful meals
    * Movement blocks
    * Evening wind-down

2. Weekly practices:
    * Technology sabbath
    * Nature immersion
    * Creative expression
    * Community connection

Action Steps

1. Immediate changes:
    * Set presence reminders
    * Create tech boundaries
    * Schedule being on time
    * Design a morning ritual

2. Weekly integration:
    * Review balance
    * Adjust routines
    * Note improvements
    * Plan next week

Remember: Balance is dynamic, not static. Adjust your approach based on energy, circumstances, and inner wisdom.

7
Empowering Choices

Maya slammed the car door shut, her heart racing with frustration and anger. The meeting with her boss had not gone well – once again, she'd been passed over for a promotion, watching the opportunity go to a less qualified colleague. As she navigated the congested streets, her mind churned with resentment and victimhood. "It's not fair," she muttered under her breath. "No matter how hard I work, I never get ahead. The deck is just stacked against me."

As Maya rehashed the injustice, her body tightened with stress – jaw clenched, shoulders hunched, breath shallow. She arrived home drained and demoralized, collapsing on the couch in a fog of hopelessness. "What's the point of even trying?" she thought bitterly. "I'm powerless to change anything. I might as well just accept my lousy lot in life."

Maya's story captures a pervasive human pattern – the tendency to feel victimized by our circumstances, to believe that life is happening to us rather than for us. Trapped in reactivity, we rail against the unfairness of it all, blaming external forces for our suffering. We feel powerless to change our situation, resigned to a fate beyond our control.

This victim mentality is a recipe for chronic stress and unhappiness. When we see ourselves as pawns at the mercy of circumstance, we live in a perpetual state of anxiety and resentment. Our nervous system gets hijacked by a sense of threat, flooding the body with stress hormones that undermine our well-being. We feel disconnected from our innate agency and creativity, unable to imagine possibilities beyond our current predicament.

At the core of this disempowered stance is a fundamental misunderstanding of the nature of choice. We falsely believe that our only options are either to passively accept things as they are or futilely fight against them. We overlook the most essential choice of all – our ability to consciously select our inner state in any given moment.

The truth is, no matter what the external circumstances, we always have the freedom to choose our response. This is the core insight that psychologist and Holocaust survivor Viktor Frankl arrived at in the darkest of situations: "Everything can be taken from a man but one thing: the last of the human freedoms — to choose one's attitude in any given set of circumstances, to choose one's own way."

Radical Responsibility

Embracing this essential freedom requires a radical shift from victimhood to self-responsibility. It means recognizing that while we may not be able to control what happens to us, we can always control how we relate to it. We move from being at the mercy of life's ups and downs to being the creative author of our inner world.

This is not to minimize the very real challenges and injustices we face, nor to suggest that we're to blame for our suffering. It's not about denying our pain or putting on a happy face in the midst of hardship. Rather, it's about empowering ourselves to consciously navigate life's difficulties with resilience and grace.

Self-responsibility begins with self-awareness – the willingness to bring mindful attention to our moment-to-moment experience. Instead of getting lost in reactive patterns, we learn to observe our thoughts and feelings with curiosity and compassion. We notice when we're slipping into victimhood and gently remind ourselves of our power to choose.

This act of witnessing opens up a space between stimulus and response – a precious pause in which we can interrupt our habitual reactivity. In that space, we gain access to our innate wisdom and creativity. We're able to ask empowering questions like: "What is this situation inviting me to learn? How can I use this challenge to grow and evolve? What choice can I make right now that aligns with my deepest values?"

From this place of self-inquiry, we start to see possibilities where before there was only a problem. We tap into our capacity to reframe adversity as an opportunity for growth and transformation. Even in the most difficult circumstances, we discover our ability to choose meaningful goals and take purposeful action in service of our vision.

Of course, this isn't about achieving a state of perpetual positivity or denying the reality of suffering. Challenges and setbacks are an inevitable part of the human journey. Self-responsibility simply means meeting those challenges with an empowered, growth-oriented mindset – and extending compassion to ourselves when we inevitably stumble.

It's also important to recognize that choice is not always comfortable or easy. Often, taking responsibility for our lives means making difficult decisions and facing our fears head-on. It requires the courage to step outside our comfort zone, to risk failure and rejection in pursuit of what matters most. Authentic empowerment demands that we take bold, decisive action – even when every fibre of our being wants to shrink back into safety.

Practices for Self-Empowerment

Cultivating this capacity for empowered choice is a lifelong practice, one that unfolds moment by moment. It begins with setting a clear intention to take responsibility for our inner world, no matter what's happening around us. By reaffirming this commitment each day, we gradually strengthen the mental and emotional muscles of self-mastery.

A key practice is to pay attention to our language and self-talk. The words we use to describe our experience have a profound impact on our perception and behaviour. When we speak in disempowering ways – "I can't," "I have to," "If only" – we reinforce a sense of helplessness and limitation. But when we choose empowering language – "I can," "I choose to," "I am" – we tap into our innate agency and strength.

Another powerful tool is reframing – the art of consciously shifting our perspective to find the opportunity in every difficulty. By asking questions like "What can I learn from this?" or "How can I use this to become a better version of myself?", we move from a victim mindset to a growth mindset. We start to see challenges as springboards for self-discovery and transformation.

Cultivating gratitude is another essential practice for self-empowerment. When we focus on what we appreciate about our lives, we shift out of scarcity and lack and into a state of abundance and sufficiency. We direct our attention towards what's working rather than what's missing, training the mind to scan for positivity and possibility. Over time, this grateful outlook becomes our default way of relating to life.

It's also crucial to surround ourselves with supportive, empowering relationships. The people we spend time with have an enormous influence on our mindset and behaviour. By seeking out others who model self-responsibility and inspire us to be our best selves, we create an environment that nourishes our growth. At the same time, we may need to lovingly distance ourselves from relationships that reinforce victimhood and disempowerment.

Perhaps most importantly, self-empowerment requires a daily practice of self-love and self-care. When we treat ourselves with compassion and respect, we send a powerful message that we are worthy of empowered choices. By tending to our physical, mental, and emotional needs, we create a strong foundation for resilient, responsible living.

As we practice self-empowerment in these ways, a profound shift starts to happen. We begin to see life not as a series of random events but as a purposeful unfolding, rich with meaning and possibility. We recognize every challenge as a call to grow, every setback as a chance to deepen our wisdom and strength. Empowered choice becomes our way of life, our default mode of operating in the world.

From Stress to Strength

This shift has profound implications for our relationship with stress. When we embrace self-responsibility, we move from a state of chronic tension to one of resilient strength. Instead of feeling constantly threatened by life's uncertainties, we develop an unshakeable inner core – a place of calm abiding in the midst of change.

his isn't to say that stress disappears altogether. Challenges and pressures are an inevitable part of the human journey. But when we meet those challenges with an empowered mindset, they lose their power to overwhelm us. We're able to stay centred in our deepest values, making choices that align with our authentic selves.

Moreover, self-responsibility allows us to proactively shape our lives in stress-reducing ways. We're able to set clear boundaries, communicate our needs assertively, and make self-honouring choices about how we spend our time and energy. We take charge of our self-care, prioritizing rest, play, and connection as essential ingredients for a life well-lived.

As we step into our power in these ways, we inspire others to do the same. Our very presence becomes a beacon of possibility, reminding those around us of their own innate freedom and agency. We become leaders in our own lives and in our communities, modelling what it looks like to live with integrity and purpose.

Self-Leadership as a Path of Service

Ultimately, self-responsibility is not just a personal practice but a form of sacred activism. When we take charge of our inner world, we become agents of change in the outer world. We bring our most resourceful, resilient selves to the challenges of our time, contributing our unique gifts in service of the greater good.

In a world plagued by stress, anxiety, and overwhelm, empowered choice is a revolutionary act. By refusing to play the victim and instead claiming our creative power, we become part of the solution. We model a way of being that is grounded in love, trust, and possibility – even in the face of great uncertainty.

At the deepest level, self-responsibility is a recognition of our fundamental interconnectedness. When we take ownership of our choices and their consequences, we acknowledge our role in the larger web of life. We see that our thoughts, words, and actions ripple out in all directions, shaping the collective reality we inhabit.

From this understanding, empowered choice becomes an act of love – for ourselves, for others, and for the world. By embracing our agency and using it wisely, we become conscious co-creators of a reality that works for all. We step into our rightful place as stewards of life, tending to the sacred unfolding with reverence and care.

An Invitation to Choose

Dear friend, I invite you to embrace the transformative power of choice in your own life. Begin by setting a clear intention to take responsibility for your inner world, no matter what's happening around you. Affirm your commitment to self-leadership, to being the author of your own story.

Notice when you're slipping into victim mentality and gently remind yourself of your power to choose. Pause in that space between stimulus and response, and ask yourself: "What is the most empowering choice I can make right now? What action aligns with my deepest values and vision?"

Practice reframing challenges as opportunities for growth and learning. Look for the gift in every struggle, the wisdom in every setback. Ask yourself what the situation is inviting you to let go of or embrace more fully.

Surround yourself with people and environments that support your empowerment. Seek out mentors, allies, and communities that inspire you to live your truth and claim your creative potential. At the same time, be willing to lovingly disengage from relationships that reinforce smallness and struggle.

Above all, treat yourself with the utmost compassion and respect. Honour your needs, your boundaries, your values. Make self-care a sacred priority, tending to your physical, emotional, and spiritual well-being with devotion. Remember that you deserve to live a life of purpose, joy, and meaning – and that it all starts with the choices you make every day.

As you walk this path of empowered living, be gentle with yourself. Self-responsibility is a practice, not a destination. There will be times when you forget your power, when you fall back into old patterns of victimhood and reactivity. In those moments, simply forgive yourself and begin again. Use your missteps as opportunities to deepen your self-compassion and renew your commitment to growth.

And always remember: You are not alone on this journey. You are part of a global awakening, a movement of souls reclaiming their creative power and using it in service of life. Every choice you make matters, every step you take contributes to the healing and transformation of our world.

So choose wisely, dear one. Choose love over fear, presence over distraction, integrity over compromise. Choose to be the change you wish to see, to embody the world you long to inhabit. And trust that life will meet you every step of the way, conspiring on your behalf to co-create a reality beyond your wildest dreams.

Empowering Choices – Practical Takeaways

Cultivating Self-Responsibility

1. Daily practices:
   * Monitor victim language
   * Notice blame patterns
   * Track reactive triggers
   * Practice pause before response

2. Empowering mindset:
   * Question limiting beliefs
   * Challenge negative assumptions
   * Look for growth opportunities
   * Reframe challenges as lessons

Making Conscious Choices

1. Decision framework:

* Align with core values
* Consider long-term impact
* Check internal motivation
* Evaluate available options

2. Response strategies:
   * Use the pause technique
   * Question initial reactions
   * Consider multiple perspectives
   * Choose conscious responses

Taking Empowered Action

1. Setting boundaries:
   * Define personal limits
   * Communicate needs clearly
   * Honour commitments to self
   * Practice saying no

2. Building momentum:
   * Start with small wins
   * Create accountability
   * Document progress
   * Celebrate successes

Creating Support Systems

1. Environmental design:

* Organize empowering spaces
* Limit exposure to negativity
* Create success reminders
* Structure for good choices

2. Relationship cultivation:
    * Connect with positive influences
    * Find accountability partners
    * Share goals and progress
    * Seek mentorship

Action Steps

1. Immediate changes:
    * Monitor self-talk
    * Practice the pause
    * Set one boundary
    * Make one empowered choice

2. Weekly practice:
    * Review response patterns
    * Assess choice alignment
    * Adjust support systems
    * Plan next steps

Remember: Every moment offers a fresh choice. Start small and build your "choice muscle" gradually.

8
Natural Vitality

Sophia woke up to the sound of birds singing outside her window, the first rays of sunlight filtering through the curtains. She stretched luxuriously, feeling the cool cotton sheets against her skin. Rolling over, she reached for her phone out of habit – but then paused, remembering her intention to start the day differently.

Instead of diving into emails and social media, Sophia took a deep breath and placed her hand on her heart. She tuned into the gentle rhythm of her heartbeat, feeling a sense of gratitude wash over her. "Thank you for this new day," she whispered. "May I live it with presence, purpose, and joy."

Rising from bed, Sophia made her way to the kitchen and prepared a nourishing breakfast – a colourful array of fresh fruits, whole grains, and healthy proteins. As she savoured each bite, she marvelled at the vibrant flavours and textures, appreciating the earth's bounty. She sipped her tea slowly, relishing the warmth and aroma.

After breakfast, Sophia stepped outside for a morning walk in the nearby park. As she strolled along the tree-lined paths, she breathed deeply, filling her lungs with the crisp, clean air. She noticed the way the sunlight danced through the leaves, casting playful shadows on the ground. She felt her body come alive with each step, her muscles and joints loosening up, her energy rising.

Returning home, Sophia took a refreshing shower and then settled onto her meditation cushion. She closed her eyes and brought her attention to her breath, observing the gentle rise and fall of her belly. When thoughts arose, she noted them kindly and then released them, coming back to the anchor of her breath. After twenty minutes, she emerged feeling clear, centred, and ready for the day ahead.

As Sophia moved through her work and responsibilities, she carried this quality of mindful presence with her. She focused on one task at a time, giving it her full care and attention. When stress or overwhelm arose, she paused to take a few conscious breaths, reconnecting with her inner calm. She made time for short stretching breaks and walking meetings, honouring her body's need for movement.

In the evening, Sophia prepared a simple, wholesome dinner, enjoying the process of chopping, sautéing, and seasoning. She ate slowly, without distractions, savouring the nourishing meal. After dinner, she spent some time on a creative hobby, losing herself in the joy of making something with her hands.

Before bed, Sophia took a warm bath infused with essential oils, allowing the day's tensions to melt away. She read a few pages of an inspiring book, filling her mind with uplifting ideas. As she drifted off to sleep, she again placed her hand on her heart, feeling a deep sense of peace and wholeness. "Thank you for this amazing day," she whispered. "May I greet tomorrow with the same presence and grace."

Sophia's story illustrates a day in the life of natural vitality – a way of living that honours the body's innate wisdom and supports our physical, mental, and emotional well-being. It's a way of relating to ourselves and the world that is grounded in presence, reverence, and joy – qualities that are our birthright but often get lost in the stress and distractions of modern life.

At the heart of natural vitality is a recognition of the deep interconnectedness of all things. We are not separate from nature but an integral part of it – our bodies a microcosm of the earth's beauty, resilience, and regenerative power. When we live in alignment with nature's rhythms and wisdom, we tap into a boundless source of energy, creativity, and healing.

The Wisdom of the Body

This alignment begins with honouring the body as a sacred vessel, a divine technology for experiencing and expressing life. So often in our fast-paced, disembodied culture, we relate to the body as a machine to be fuelled, pushed, and manipulated to serve our agendas. We override its natural signals with caffeine, junk food, and electronic stimulation. We numb its aches and pains with pills and distraction, soldiering on in the name of productivity.

But this disconnection from the body's wisdom comes at a steep cost. When we chronically ignore or suppress our physical needs, we set the stage for stress, burnout, and disease. We cut ourselves off from our innate vitality and end up dragging ourselves through the day, running on empty.

The path of natural vitality invites us to befriend the body, to listen to its messages with curiosity and respect. It means attuning to the body's subtle cues – hunger, thirst, fatigue, restlessness – and responding with loving care. Instead of seeing the body as a problem to be fixed, we learn to trust its ancient intelligence, cooperating with its natural impulse towards balance and health.

This shift in perspective has profound implications for our relationship with food, movement, rest, and self-care. Instead of imposing rigid regimens based on external ideals, we tune into our unique needs and preferences, honouring what truly nourishes us on all levels. We discover the power of intuitive eating, mindful movement, and restorative practices as pathways to wholeness.

As we deepen our embodied presence, we start to experience the body as a portal to the sacred – a way of directly savouring the beauty and mystery of life. Each sensation becomes an invitation to awe, from the pulsing vitality of a grounding walk to the delicious pleasure of a ripe peach. We fall in love with the simple miracle of breathing, the steady rhythm that connects us to all of life.

The Nourishment of Nature

This embodied reverence naturally extends to the larger rhythms and cycles of the earth. We recognize that our well-being is intimately tied to that of the planet – that we are part of a vast, intelligent web of life. Just as the body thrives on wholesome food, fresh air, and clean water, our souls are fed by the beauty and wonder of the natural world.

Spending time in nature is one of the most powerful ways to cultivate natural vitality. When we immerse ourselves in wild landscapes – forests, mountains, oceans, rivers – we sync up with the earth's healing frequencies, allowing our nervous systems to relax and reset. We remember our place in the larger web of life, shedding the illusion of separation and control.

Nature also teaches us about the wisdom of cycles and seasons. Just as the earth moves through periods of growth, fruition, release, and renewal, our own lives unfold in organic rhythms of activity and rest. When we attune to these natural flows – honouring our need for both doing and being, striving and surrender – we access a deep wellspring of vitality.

This means embracing the gifts of each season, both inner and outer. In spring, we plant seeds of intention and nurture new growth. In summer, we savour the fruits of our labours and celebrate the fullness of life. In autumn, we release what no longer serves and make space for what's to come. And in winter, we turn inward, slowing down to rest and reflect.

By aligning with these cyclical rhythms, we tap into a source of enduring energy and creativity. We learn to pace ourselves for the long haul, balancing periods of intense activity with times of rest and regeneration. We honour the natural ebb and flow of our energy levels, working with rather than against our body's needs.

Creativity and Play

Another key ingredient of natural vitality is making space for creativity and play. In our productivity-obsessed culture, we often view these pursuits as frivolous extras – activities to be squeezed in if and when we have time. But creative expression and joyful play are actually essential nutrients for the soul, fuelling our vitality and resilience in powerful ways.

When we engage in activities that light us up from the inside out, we tap into a wellspring of renewable energy. Whether it's painting, dancing, singing, gardening, or tinkering with a beloved hobby, creativity connects us with our innate sense of wonder and possibility. It shifts us out of our rational, linear minds and into a state of flow and timelessness.

Play serves a similar function, reminding us of the sheer delight of being alive. When we let ourselves be silly, spontaneous, and fully present in the moment, we release stress and tension from the body. We access a childlike sense of joy and freedom that is deeply restorative for the nervous system.

Making time for these soul-nourishing activities is not a luxury but a necessity for vibrant living. Even a few minutes a day of creative expression or playful movement can have a profound impact on our overall well-being. It's a way of sending a message to ourselves that our wholeness matters, that we are worthy of joy and delight.

Sacred Self-Care

At its core, natural vitality is a practice of radical self-love – of treating ourselves with the same tenderness and care we would offer a beloved child or cherished friend. It means making our own well-being a sacred priority, tending to our physical, emotional, and spiritual needs with devotion.

This kind of self-care goes beyond bubble baths and dark chocolate (though those are wonderful too!). It's a daily practice of tuning into our authentic needs and honouring them with loving action. It means setting healthy boundaries, saying no to what depletes us and yes to what nourishes us. It means carving out time for rest, reflection, and renewal, even in the midst of a busy life.

Importantly, sacred self-care is not about perfection or indulgence. It's not another item on our to-do list or a way to earn love and acceptance. Rather, it's a gentle, compassionate way of relating to ourselves moment to moment – a recognition that we are worthy of care and kindness simply because we exist.

As we cultivate this loving presence towards ourselves, we naturally start to make more nourishing choices in all areas of life. We gravitate towards wholesome foods, invigorating movement, and uplifting relationships. We create environments that support our well-being, surrounding ourselves with beauty, inspiration, and healing energy.

Living in Alignment

Ultimately, natural vitality is about living in alignment with our deepest values and truest selves. It's about creating a life that honours our authentic needs and desires, that expresses our unique gifts and passions. When we are in integrity with our essential nature, we experience a profound sense of ease, flow, and purposefulness.

This kind of alignment requires listening deeply to the whispers of our soul – the quiet longings, the subtle nudges, the fleeting moments of inspiration. It means following our curiosity and excitement, even when it leads us off the beaten path. It means trusting our intuition and inner wisdom, even in the face of fear or uncertainty.

As we align our lives with our heart's deepest truth, we tap into a renewable source of vitality and meaning. We become a clear channel for the life force to flow through us, expressing itself in ways that are unique to our gifts and callings. Our very presence becomes a healing force, inspiring others to live more fully and authentically.

Of course, living in alignment is not always easy or comfortable. It requires courage, vulnerability, and a willingness to let go of what no longer serves. It means facing our shadows and fears, shedding old patterns and beliefs that keep us small and stuck. It means taking risks and leaping into the unknown, trusting that life will catch us.

But the rewards of this path are immeasurable. When we live in alignment with our deepest truth, we experience a sense of wholeness and purpose that is unshakeable. We tap into a wellspring of natural vitality that sustains us through life's challenges and uncertainties. And we become a force for healing and transformation in the world, simply by being who we truly are.

An Invitation to Vitality

Dear friend, I invite you to embrace the path of natural vitality – to honour your body's wisdom, to align with nature's rhythms, to nourish your soul with creativity and play, to tend to your needs with sacred self-care. I invite you to listen deeply to your heart's whispers and follow your authentic path, even when it leads you into uncharted territory.

Know that this path is not about reaching some distant goal or ideal but about falling in love with the sacred journey of life itself. It's about savouring the simple miracles of each moment – the breath in your lungs, the sun on your face, the laughter of a loved one. It's about celebrating your own unique beauty and gifts, knowing that the world needs your light.

As you walk this path, be gentle and patient with yourself. Remember that natural vitality is not a destination but a daily choice, a moment-to-moment practice of loving presence. There will be times when you forget, when you fall back into old patterns of stress and depletion. In those moments, simply begin again, with compassion and grace.

Trust that your body is wise, that it knows the way back to wholeness. Listen to its messages and honour its needs, even when it asks you to slow down or let go. Surround yourself with beauty, inspiration, and loving support, creating an environment that nourishes your soul. And above all, stay true to your own authentic path, knowing that it will lead you home to yourself.

May your journey be filled with wonder, joy, and boundless vitality. May you awaken to the magic and mystery of life in every moment. And may you know yourself as a radiant embodiment of nature's beauty, resilience, and grace.

Natural Vitality – Practical Takeaways

Body Connection

1. Daily body awareness:
    * Morning body scan
    * Regular energy check-ins
    * Hunger/thirst monitoring
    * Body signals tracking

2. Mindful movement:
    * Regular stretching breaks
    * Nature walks
    * Intuitive exercise
    * Gentle yoga/movement

Natural Rhythms

1. Seasonal alignment:
    * Adjust activities to seasons
    * Follow natural light cycles
    * Align food choices seasonally
    * Honour energy fluctuations

2. Daily rhythms:
    * Morning sunlight exposure
    * Regular meal times
    * Evening wind-down routine
    * Consistent sleep schedule

Nourishment Practices

1. Mindful eating:
    * Regular, balanced meals
    * Eating without distractions
    * Food preparation rituals
    * Hydration awareness

2. Environmental nourishment:
    * Regular nature time
    * Fresh air exposure
    * Natural light optimization
    * Green space connection

Creative Expression

1. Daily creativity:
    * Art/music practice
    * Journaling
    * Free movement/dance
    * Creative hobbies

2. Playful living:
    * Scheduled play time
    * Spontaneous activities
    * Movement games
    * Creative exploration

Action Steps

1. Morning vitality:
    * Natural light exposure
    * Movement practice
    * Nourishing breakfast
    * Mindful moments

2. Daily integration:
    * Nature breaks
    * Creative expression
    * Body check-ins
    * Playful activities

Remember: Natural vitality emerges from aligning with your body's wisdom and nature's rhythms.

9
Love, Laughter, and Letting Go

Raj sat on the edge of his bed, his head in his hands. It had been a tough week – his project at work was behind schedule, his car had broken down, and he'd had a frustrating argument with his partner. He felt the familiar weight of stress and worry pressing down on him, a heaviness that seemed to seep into his very bones.

Just then, his phone buzzed with an incoming video call. It was his five-year-old niece, Priya, her face filling the screen with a gap-toothed grin. "Uncle Raj!" she exclaimed. "Look what I learned in school today!" She proceeded to sing the alphabet song, complete with exuberant hand motions and a few creative pronunciations.

As Raj watched Priya's joyful performance, he felt a smile spreading across his face. His shoulders relaxed, and his breathing deepened. By the time Priya finished with a flourish, Raj was laughing out loud, the stress of the week momentarily forgotten. "That was amazing, Priya!" he said. "You just made my whole day."

After the call, Raj reflected on the power of that simple moment of connection and laughter. It was like a ray of sunshine piercing through the clouds of his stress, reminding him of what truly mattered. He felt a wave of love and gratitude wash over him – for Priya, for his family, for all the blessings in his life.

With a newfound lightness, Raj decided to take a walk in the park near his house. As he strolled along the tree-lined path, he breathed in the fresh air and felt the warmth of the sun on his skin. He watched a group of children playing on the grass, their laughter echoing across the field. He marvelled at the beauty of the flowers, the intricacy of a spider's web, the easy grace of a squirrel leaping from branch to branch.

As Raj walked, he felt his perspective shifting. The challenges of the week were still there, but they no longer seemed so overwhelming. He realized that stress was not an objective reality but a function of his own thoughts and reactions. He had a choice in how he responded to life's difficulties – he could contract in fear and resistance or expand in love and acceptance.

With each step, Raj practised letting go – releasing his grip on how he thought things should be and opening to the possibilities of the present moment. He silently repeated a mantra to himself: "I surrender to the flow of life. I trust in the wisdom of the universe. I choose love over fear." He felt a sense of peace and ease wash over him, a quiet knowing that all was unfolding as it should.

The Power of Love

Raj's story illustrates the transformative power of love, laughter, and letting go. These are not just feel-good sentiments but profound spiritual practices that have the power to dissolve stress and open us to the fullness of life. When we cultivate these qualities, we tap into a source of resilience and joy that is deeper than our temporary circumstances.

At the heart of love is a recognition of our fundamental interconnectedness. We are not separate beings but expressions of a unified field of consciousness, inextricably woven into the fabric of life. When we open our hearts to this truth, we experience a profound sense of belonging and wholeness. We see that we are never truly alone, that we are held in an infinite web of relationships and care.

This kind of love is not limited to romantic partnership but encompasses all of our relationships –

with family, friends, community, and even strangers. It extends to our relationship with ourselves, as we learn to embrace all parts of our being with compassion and acceptance. And it includes our relationship with the natural world, as we recognize the earth as a living, sacred being worthy of reverence and care.

When we live from this place of love, stress naturally begins to dissolve. We no longer feel so isolated and threatened by life's challenges, but instead experience a deep sense of support and connection. We trust that we are part of a larger flow of wisdom and grace, even when we cannot see the full picture. We open to the possibility that everything is happening for our highest good, even if it doesn't feel that way in the moment.

Of course, cultivating this kind of unconditional love is a lifelong practice. It requires continually choosing to lead with the heart rather than the head, to respond to fear with compassion, to forgive ourselves and others when we fall short. It means setting healthy boundaries and speaking our truth while also staying open and receptive to others' needs and perspectives.

One powerful way to cultivate love is through the practice of loving-kindness meditation. This involves silently repeating phrases of goodwill and care, first for ourselves and then extending outward to others. We might say, "May I be filled with loving-kindness. May I be well. May I be peaceful and at ease. May I be happy." We then extend these wishes to a beloved friend, a neutral person, a challenging person, and ultimately all beings everywhere.

As we practice this kind of unconditional love, we start to see the world through new eyes. Instead of judging and comparing, we appreciate the inherent worth and beauty in all beings. We feel a sense of kinship and solidarity with the joys and sorrows of our fellow humans. Our hearts expand to include more and more of life, until we experience a love that knows no bounds.

The Gift of Laughter

Alongside love, laughter is one of the most powerful antidotes to stress. When we laugh, we release endorphins that boost our mood, relax our muscles, and strengthen our immune system. Laughter shifts our brain waves into a more relaxed and creative state, allowing us to see problems from a fresh perspective. It connects us with others and fosters a sense of playfulness and joy.

Yet in the seriousness of adult life, laughter is often in short supply. We get so caught up in our responsibilities and worries that we forget how to let go and have fun. We wear our stress like a badge of honour, as if being perpetually busy and burdened is a sign of importance and worth. We lose touch with the childlike wonder and spontaneity that is our birthright.

The path of natural vitality invites us to reclaim the gift of laughter, to make space for lightheartedness and play. It means seeking out experiences and relationships that bring us joy, that tickle our funny bone and light us up from the inside. It means learning to take ourselves less seriously, to find the humour and absurdity in even the most challenging situations.

One way to cultivate more laughter is to surround ourselves with people who know how to have fun. Whether it's joining a laughter yoga class, attending a comedy show, or simply spending time with friends who make us smile, we can intentionally seek out environments that foster lightness and levity. We can also practice finding the humour in everyday moments, looking for opportunities to be silly and playful.

Another powerful practice is to engage in activities that bring us into a state of flow and timelessness. When we are fully absorbed in a creative pursuit or physical activity that we love, our worries and stresses naturally fall away. We enter a state of joyful presence, where the mind quiets and the soul sings. Whether it's dancing, painting, hiking, or playing music, finding our flow is a direct route to more laughter and ease.

Ultimately, laughter is a choice – a way of relating to life that is open, curious, and unattached. It's a recognition that even in the midst of challenges and difficulties, there is always room for a moment of levity, a spark of joy. As the Yiddish proverb says, "What soap is to the body, laughter is to the soul." By bringing more laughter into our lives, we cleanse ourselves of stress and open ourselves to the fresh possibilities of the present moment.

The Freedom of Letting Go

Embedded in both love and laughter is a profound practice of letting go. When we are caught in the grip of stress, we are usually holding on tightly to something – a desired outcome, a fear of failure, a need for control. We clench our minds and bodies in resistance to what is, fighting against the natural flow of life. This creates immense tension and suffering, as we exhaust ourselves trying to manipulate reality to fit our expectations.

The path of letting go invites us to relax our grip, to surrender our agenda and open to the wisdom of the present moment. It means releasing our attachment to how we think things should be and cultivating a deeper trust in the unfolding of life. It means learning to ride the waves of change with grace and flexibility, rather than getting tossed around by our own rigidity.

This kind of letting go is not a passive resignation but an active choice to align ourselves with what is. It's a recognition that our true power lies not in control but in acceptance, not in resistance but in flow. When we let go of our limited ideas of how life should be, we open ourselves to the infinite possibilities of how life could be. We become co-creators with the universe, partners in the dynamic dance of existence.

One powerful practice of letting go is mindfulness meditation. By bringing our attention to the present moment, we learn to observe our thoughts and feelings without getting caught up in them. We see that our stressful experiences are not solid realities but passing phenomena, arising and dissolving like clouds in the sky. As we cultivate this kind of non-attached awareness, we naturally begin to loosen our grip on our ego-driven agendas.

Another key practice is self-compassion. When we are stressed, we often add to our suffering by judging and criticizing ourselves. We get caught up in a spiral of negative self-talk, blaming ourselves for our difficulties and perceived shortcomings. Self-compassion invites us to let go of this inner harshness and extend kindness and understanding to ourselves. It means treating ourselves with the same care and concern we would offer a good friend, recognizing our common humanity.

As we practice letting go in these ways, we start to experience a profound sense of freedom and ease. We no longer feel so burdened by the weight of our expectations and judgements, but instead rest in the spaciousness of the present moment. We trust that we have the resilience and resourcefulness to meet life's challenges as they arise, without getting overwhelmed or reactive. We experience a deep sense of flow and alignment, a knowing that we are exactly where we need to be.

Living in Love

Ultimately, love, laughter, and letting go are invitations to live in alignment with our deepest nature. They remind us that beneath the stress and struggle of the human experience, there is a wellspring of joy, creativity, and connection that is always available to us. When we tap into these qualities, we come home to ourselves and to the world around us.

This is not a one-time event but a daily practice, a continual choice to meet life with an open and tender heart. It means cultivating moments of love and laughter throughout our day, even in the midst of busyness and challenges. It means practising letting go again and again, releasing our resistance to the present moment and opening to the fresh possibilities of the Now.

As we live in this way, we naturally begin to radiate a quality of presence that is deeply nourishing to ourselves and others. We become a force for love in the world, not through grand gestures but through the way we show up in each interaction, each breath. Our very being becomes a reminder of the beauty and sacredness of life, a living invitation to embrace the fullness of the human experience.

Of course, this path is not always easy. There will be times when fear and stress override our best intentions, when we forget our innate wholeness and get caught up in the drama of the mind. In these moments, the practice is to bring compassion to our experience, to lovingly remind ourselves of who we really are. We dust ourselves off, recommit to our intention, and begin again.

The good news is that we are not alone on this path. We are part of a growing community of beings who are awakening to a new way of living, one rooted in love, joy, and mindful presence. By supporting and inspiring each other, we create a field of collective transformation, a web of light that is healing our world from the inside out.

So let us practice, dear friends – with dedication, with humour, with infinite gentleness. Let us embrace the moments of love and laughter that are waiting for us in each day, and learn to let go of all that is not serving our highest good. Let us remember the sacredness of our being and live in alignment with our deepest truth. And let us trust that as we do this, we are co-creating a world of greater peace, connection, and aliveness for all beings.

Love, Laughter, and Letting Go – Practical Takeaways

Cultivating Love

1. Daily love practices:
    * Loving-kindness meditation
    * Gratitude journaling
    * Random acts of kindness
    * Self-compassion breaks

2. Relationship building:
    * Quality time with loved ones
    * Active listening
    * Expressing appreciation
    * Practising forgiveness

Embracing Laughter

1. Daily joy practices:
    * Playful movement
    * Humour breaks
    * Creative expression
    * Light-hearted activities

2. Social connection:
    * Time with uplifting people
    * Sharing funny moments

* Group activities
* Play dates

Letting Go

1. Release practices:
    * Mindful breathing
    * Body scanning
    * Journaling
    * Nature walks

2. Surrender tools:
    * Non-attachment exercises
    * Acceptance phrases
    * Release rituals
    * Trust building

Integration Practices

1. Morning routine:
    * Gratitude practice
    * Joy movement
    * Release meditation
    * Heart connection

2. Throughout the day:
    * Mindful pauses
    * Laughter breaks

* Love notes
* Let go moments

Action Steps

1. Daily integration:
    * Choose one love practice
    * Schedule joy time
    * Practice letting go
    * Connect with others

2. Weekly review:
    * Note moments of joy
    * Track stress releases
    * Plan connection time
    * Adjust practices

Remember: These practices work together to create a foundation of resilience and ease.

10
From Stress to Serenity

Maria stood at the edge of the ocean, her feet sinking into the soft sand as the waves lapped gently around her ankles. The sun was just starting to peek over the horizon, painting the sky in swirls of pink and orange. She closed her eyes and took a deep breath, savouring the salty tang of the air, the cool caress of the breeze on her skin.

As Maria breathed, she felt a sense of peace wash over her – a deep, abiding stillness that seemed to emanate from her very core. It was a feeling she had once thought impossible, a state of being that had eluded her for most of her life. For as long as she could remember, stress had been her constant companion – a nagging undercurrent of anxiety and tension that coloured her every experience.

But now, as she stood at the edge of this vast, unknowable ocean, Maria realized that something had shifted within her. The stress was still there, but it no longer consumed her. She could observe it with a sense of curiosity and detachment, without getting caught up in its tumultuous currents. She had discovered a place of serenity within herself, a calm centre from which she could weather any storm.

This transformation had not happened overnight. It was the fruit of a long and sometimes arduous journey – a path of self-discovery and inner growth that had asked her to confront her deepest fears and beliefs. Along the way, Maria had learned to cultivate new habits and perspectives, to let go of old patterns that no longer served her. She had come to understand that stress was not an external force to be conquered, but an internal response that she could learn to befriend and transform.

As the sun rose higher in the sky, casting a golden glow over the water, Maria reflected on the key insights and practices that had brought her to this place of peace. She knew that her journey was far from over – that there would always be new challenges and opportunities for growth. But she also knew that she had found a compass to guide her – an inner wisdom that would lead her home to herself, again and again.

The Roots of Serenity

At the heart of Maria's transformation was a shift in her understanding of the nature of stress and serenity. She had once seen these states as opposites – as mutually exclusive experiences that could never coexist. Stress was the enemy, something to be vanquished or avoided at all costs. Serenity was a distant dream, a state of perfect calm that was always just out of reach.

But as Maria delved deeper into the wisdom traditions of the world, she began to see stress and serenity in a new light. She realized that these experiences were not separate but intimately interconnected – two sides of the same coin, two faces of the same reality. Stress was simply the mind's resistance to what is, a contraction against the present moment. Serenity was the natural state of the mind when it let go of this resistance, when it opened to the fullness of life as it unfolded.

This understanding echoed the teachings of the great spiritual masters throughout history. The Buddha taught that suffering arises from attachment – from clinging to our desires and aversions, our ideas of how things should be. Jesus spoke of the peace that surpasses understanding, a state of grace that arises when we surrender our will to the will of God. The Tao Te Ching speaks of the way of wu wei, the path of effortless action that comes from aligning ourselves with the natural flow of life.

At their core, these teachings point to a fundamental truth: that serenity is not something we can achieve through effort or willpower, but something we uncover through letting go. It is the natural state of our being, the calm centre that is always present beneath the turbulence of our thoughts and emotions. When we learn to rest in this centre, to abide in the stillness of our own awareness, we discover a peace that is unshakeable, a joy that is not contingent on external circumstances.

This is not to say that the path to serenity is a path of passivity or resignation. On the contrary, it is a path of profound engagement and aliveness – a path that asks us to show up fully for the reality of each moment, to meet life with an open and courageous heart. It is a path of inner work and outer action, of self-inquiry and compassionate service. But it is a path that is rooted in a deep trust in the fundamental goodness of life, a recognition that beneath the chaos and confusion of the world, there is an underlying order and intelligence that is always guiding us towards growth and healing.

The Practice of Presence

One of the key practices that Maria learned on her journey to serenity was the art of mindfulness – the simple yet profound act of bringing her attention to the present moment, without judgement or resistance. She discovered that when she was fully present, fully engaged in the reality of her experience, stress naturally began to dissolve. She was no longer caught up in the stories of her mind, the endless loop of worries and regrets, but resting in the spaciousness of her own awareness.

At first, this practice felt foreign and uncomfortable. Maria's mind was so used to being in constant motion, always racing towards the next goal or problem to be solved. Sitting still and observing her thoughts felt like trying to tame a wild horse – every time she brought her attention to her breath, her mind would gallop off in another direction, chasing after some new distraction or worry.

But with time and patience, Maria began to develop a new relationship with her mind. She learned to watch her thoughts and emotions with a sense of curiosity and detachment, without getting caught up in their drama. She discovered that her awareness was like a vast sky – no matter how many clouds of thought passed through, the sky itself remained unchanged, untouched by their passing.

As Maria practised mindfulness in her daily life, she started to notice subtle shifts in her experience. She became more attuned to the sensations of her body, the rhythm of her breath, the play of light and shadow in the world around her. She found herself savouring simple moments that she had once rushed past – the warmth of a cup of tea in her hands, the laughter of a child in the park, the quiet beauty of a sunset over the city skyline.

She also began to catch herself more quickly when she slipped into old patterns of stress and reactivity. Instead of getting swept away by a wave of anger or anxiety, she learned to pause and take a conscious breath, to feel the energy of the emotion without being consumed by it. She discovered that by bringing a kind and gentle attention to her inner world, she could create a space of choice and freedom, a place from which she could respond to life's challenges with greater wisdom and care.

The Power of Letting Go

As Maria deepened her practice of mindfulness, she also began to confront the many ways in which she was holding on to stress – the beliefs, patterns, and habits that were keeping her trapped in a state of tension and unease. She realized that much of her suffering came not from the challenges of life itself, but from her resistance to those challenges, her insistence that things should be other than they were.

One of the most powerful beliefs that Maria had to let go of was the idea that her worth was contingent on her achievements, her status, and her ability to please others. For so long, she had driven herself relentlessly, always striving to prove her value through external accomplishments. She had based her identity on being the perfect employee, the perfect friend, the perfect partner – always putting others' needs before her own, always pushing herself to do more and be more.

But as Maria began to practice self-inquiry and self-compassion, she started to see the toll that this belief was taking on her well-being. She realized that her constant striving was actually a form of self-violence, a way of telling herself that she was not enough just as she was. She saw how much energy she was wasting in trying to control the perceptions of others, how much of her life she was missing in her quest for validation and approval.

Slowly, with great tenderness and care, Maria began to let go of this belief. She started to treat herself with the same kindness and understanding that she would offer a dear friend. She learned to set boundaries and say no when she needed to, to honour her own needs and desires without guilt or apology. She began to see her worth as inherent, not something that needed to be earned or proven.

As Maria let go of this old belief, she felt a profound sense of liberation and relief. It was as if a great weight had been lifted from her shoulders, a weight that she had been carrying for so long that she had forgotten it was there. She felt a new sense of lightness and ease, a freedom to be herself without the constant pressure to perform or impress.

This process of letting go was not a one-time event, but a daily practice – a continual choice to release the thoughts and patterns that were no longer serving her. Maria learned to be patient and compassionate with herself, to recognize that old habits sometimes resurfaced in times of stress or uncertainty. But she also learned to trust in her own resilience, her ability to meet each moment with fresh eyes and an open heart.

Cultivating Connection

As Maria continued on her journey to serenity, she also began to recognize the vital importance of connection – the deep sense of belonging and interdependence that is our birthright as human beings. She saw how much of her stress and anxiety came from a sense of isolation and separation, a feeling that she was alone in her struggles and challenges.

Maria started to cultivate a new kind of relationship with herself – one based on curiosity, acceptance, and care. She learned to listen to her body's wisdom, to honour its needs for rest and nourishment. She began to treat her thoughts and emotions with respect, not as enemies to be conquered but as messengers to be heard and understood. She discovered a deep wellspring of inner strength and resilience, a core of unshakeable peace that was always available to her.

At the same time, Maria also began to reach out to others in a new way – not from a place of neediness or desperation, but from a place of wholeness and generosity. She started to share her own struggles and vulnerabilities with trusted friends and loved ones, and found that this honesty and openness invited a new depth of connection and support. She discovered the healing power of being seen and heard, of knowing that she was not alone in her human experience.

Maria also began to connect with something greater than herself – a sense of purpose and meaning that transcended her individual life. She volunteered at a local shelter, offering comfort and care to those who were struggling. She joined a meditation group, sitting in silence with others who shared her commitment to inner growth and transformation. She spent time in nature, marvelling at the beauty and intelligence of the living world around her.

Through these experiences of connection, Maria felt a profound sense of belonging and wholeness. She realized that she was part of a vast web of life, a tapestry of relationships and interdependencies that stretched far beyond her individual self. She saw that her own journey to serenity was not separate from the journey of others, but intimately woven together in a great dance of healing and awakening.

Living in Alignment

As Maria integrated these practices and insights into her daily life, she began to experience a profound shift in her relationship to stress and serenity. She no longer saw these states as enemies to be conquered, but as beloved teachers and guides – invitations to deeper awareness, greater compassion, and more authentic living.

She discovered that true serenity was not a static state of bliss, but a dynamic dance of engagement and release, of coming home to oneself again and again in each moment. She learned to welcome stress as a signal that something within her was out of alignment – a call to pause, to listen, to adjust her course with wisdom and care.

Maria also began to see that her own journey to serenity was not just a personal quest, but a way of contributing to the healing of the world. She saw how much of the suffering and conflict in the world came from the same roots of fear, separation, and resistance that had once dominated her own life. She realized that by practising mindfulness, compassion, and connection in her own life, she was helping to create a more peaceful and loving world for all beings.

As she stood at the edge of the ocean that morning, Maria felt a deep sense of gratitude and awe for the journey that had brought her to this place. She knew that there would always be new challenges and opportunities for growth, new invitations to let go and open to the fullness of life. But she also knew that she had found a path of the heart, a way of living that was aligned with her deepest values and aspirations.

With a smile on her face and a lightness in her step, Maria turned and made her way back up the beach, ready to meet the new day with curiosity, courage, and an open heart. She had discovered that the path from stress to serenity was not a straight line, but a winding road of self-discovery and transformation – a journey that would continue to unfold for the rest of her life. And she couldn't wait to see where it would lead her next.

Postscript: A Call to Awakening

Dear reader,

As we come to the end of this exploration of stress and serenity, I invite you to take a moment to reflect on your own journey. What has brought you to this point in your life? What are the beliefs, patterns, and habits that have shaped your experience of stress and well-being? What are the practices and insights that have helped you find greater peace and clarity?

As you ponder these questions, remember that you are not alone. The path from stress to serenity is one that countless others have walked before you, and will continue to walk long after you. It is a path that is as unique as your own fingerprint, and yet shares a common thread with all of humanity – the longing to be free from suffering, to live with authenticity and joy, to know the deepest truth of who you are.

The journey to serenity is not always easy. It asks us to confront our deepest fears and vulnerabilities, to let go of the stories and identities that have defined us for so long. It requires us to cultivate new habits of mind and heart, to practice self-compassion and self-awareness in the face of life's challenges. It invites us to connect with others in a spirit of openness and generosity, to recognize our fundamental interdependence and shared humanity.

But for all its challenges, the path to serenity is also a path of immense beauty and grace. It is a path that leads us back to our own hearts, to the wellspring of wisdom and compassion that lies at the core of our being. It is a path that connects us with the living world around us, with the great web of life that sustains and nourishes us all. It is a path that invites us to live with purpose and meaning, to offer our unique gifts in service of something greater than ourselves.

As you embark on this path, know that you carry within you all the resources you need to find your way. Trust in your own inner wisdom, your capacity for growth and transformation. Surround yourself with people and practices that support your journey, that remind you of your inherent worth and goodness. And above all, be kind to yourself – remember that you are a work in progress, a beautiful unfolding of life in all its mystery and wonder.

The path from stress to serenity is a path of awakening – a journey from the illusion of separation to the reality of our fundamental unity. It is a path that leads us home to ourselves and to the great web of life that connects us all. May you walk this path with courage, compassion, and an open heart. May you discover the deep peace and joy that is your birthright. And may you be a light for others, a beacon of hope and healing in a world that so desperately needs it.

From Stress to Serenity – Practical Takeaways

Integrating Core Practices

1. Mindfulness foundation:
    * Regular meditation
    * Present-moment awareness

* Body scanning
* Breath awareness

2. Release techniques:
   * Stress pattern recognition
   * Conscious letting go
   * Release rituals
   * Emotional processing

Building Resilience

1. Daily practices:
   * Morning intention setting
   * Midday check-ins
   * Evening reflection
   * Gratitude moments

2. Support systems:
   * Trusted companions
   * Professional guidance
   * Community connection
   * Nature immersion

Living with Purpose

1. Alignment practices:
   * Values check-ins
   * Priority assessment

* Boundary setting
* Action alignment

2. Growth mindset:
    * Learning from challenges
    * Embracing change
    * Cultivating curiosity
    * Celebrating progress

Sustainable Integration

1. Life rhythms:
    * Work-rest balance
    * Connection time
    * Solo recharge
    * Creative expression

2. Long-term support:
    * Regular reviews
    * Practice adjustments
    * Skill development
    * Community building

Remember: The path to serenity is ongoing. Small, consistent actions create lasting transformation.

Conclusion: An Invitation to Serenity

As we come to the end of this introduction, I am filled with a sense of hope and possibility. I think back to my own journey from stress to serenity, and the many moments of struggle and awakening that have brought me to this place of deeper peace and purpose.

I remember one moment in particular, a few years ago, when I was at a crossroads in my life. I had been working tirelessly for years, pursuing success and achievement at all costs, and I had finally reached a point of exhaustion and burnout. I felt like I was drowning in stress and anxiety, disconnected from my deepest values and aspirations.

It was in that moment of despair that I had a profound realization. I saw that the path I was on was not sustainable, that it was leading me away from the very things that mattered most to me – my health, my relationships, my sense of meaning and purpose. And I knew that I had to make a change.

That change did not happen overnight. It was a gradual process of letting go of old patterns and beliefs, of cultivating new habits and perspectives. It required a deep commitment to mindfulness and self-compassion, a willingness to confront my fears and vulnerabilities with courage and grace.

But as I began to align myself with my true nature, to listen to the whispers of my heart and soul, I started to experience a profound shift. The stress and anxiety that had once consumed me began to dissolve, replaced by a sense of inner peace and clarity. I felt more connected to myself and others, more alive and awake to the beauty and possibility of each moment.

As I reflect on that journey now, I am filled with gratitude for the many teachers and guides who have supported me along the way – the mentors and friends who have shared their wisdom and compassion, the books and practices that have illuminated the path to greater well-being and resilience.

And I am filled with a deep sense of purpose and passion for sharing these insights and practices with others. Because I know that the path from stress to serenity is not just a personal journey, but a collective one, it is a path that has the power to transform not just our individual lives, but our families, our communities, and our world.

That is why I wrote this book – to offer a roadmap for that transformation, a guide to living with greater ease, joy, and purpose in a world that often feels overwhelming and uncertain. I believe that by cultivating mindfulness, compassion, and connection in ourselves and in our relationships, we have the power to create ripples of positive change that extend far beyond our individual lives.

But I also know that this path is not always easy. It requires courage and commitment, a willingness to step outside our comfort zones and embrace the full spectrum of human experience. It asks us to confront the root causes of our stress and suffering, to take responsibility for our own well-being and the well-being of others.

And yet, I believe that this path is worth it. Because the alternative – a life of chronic stress and disconnection, of endless striving and dissatisfaction – is simply too high a price to pay. We deserve to live with greater ease and joy, to experience the fullness of our humanity with all its beauty and complexity.

So, as you embark on this journey from stress to serenity, know that you are not alone. You are part of a growing community of individuals and organizations around the world who are committed to creating a more mindful, compassionate, and sustainable way of living. By cultivating these qualities in ourselves and in our communities, we have the power to create a better world for ourselves and for generations to come.

Let this book be a companion and guide on that journey. Let it be a reminder of the deep wisdom and resilience that lies within each of us, waiting to be awakened. Let it be an invitation to live with greater presence, purpose, and joy, moment by moment, day by day.

And let us remember that the path to serenity is not a destination, but a way of being in the world. It is a commitment to showing up fully for ourselves and others, to embracing the ups and downs of life with courage and compassion. It is a recognition of our fundamental interconnectedness and the power we have to create a world of greater peace, justice, and flourishing for all.

So let us begin this journey together, with open hearts and minds, ready to discover the transformative power of mindfulness, compassion, and connection. Let us support and inspire each other along the way, remembering that we are all in this together, that we are all part of a larger web of life that sustains and nourishes us.

And let us trust in the wisdom and resilience of our own hearts and minds, knowing that we have everything we need to navigate the challenges and opportunities of this precious human life. May this book be a blessing and a guide on that journey, and may it inspire us to live with greater ease, purpose, and joy, now and in all the moments to come.

With heartfelt gratitude and hope,
Dr. Jawahar Surisetti

Addendum

Internal Triggers

Thoughts/Beliefs:

1. ______________________________________
2. ______________________________________
3. ______________________________________

Expectations:

1. ______________________________________
2. ______________________________________
3. ______________________________________

Physical Factors:

1. ______________________________________
2. ______________________________________
3. ______________________________________

For Each Trigger, Rate:

- Intensity (1-10): How strongly does this affect you?
- Frequency (1-10): How often does this occur?
- Control (1-10): How much control do you have over this? (1=none, 10=complete)

3. Mind-Body Connection Self-Assessment

For each situation below, note your typical physical, emotional, and thought responses:

Situation 1: Facing a deadline
- Physical response: ______________________
- Emotional response: ______________________
- Thought patterns: ______________________

Situation 2: Conflict with someone important to you
- Physical response: ______________________
- Emotional response: ______________________
- Thought patterns: ______________________

Situation 3: Financial pressure
- Physical response: ______________________
- Emotional response: ______________________
- Thought patterns: ______________________

Situation 4: Public speaking/performance
- Physical response: ______________________
- Emotional response: ______________________
- Thought patterns: ______________________

5: Making an important decision
- Physical response: ______________________
- Emotional response: ______________________
- Thought patterns: ______________________

4. Stress Response Patterns Questionnaire

Circle the response that most closely matches your typical reaction:

1. When facing a challenging situation, I typically:
a) Confront it head-on, sometimes aggressively
b) Avoid or postpone dealing with it
c) Feel paralyzed or overwhelmed
d) Seek help or advice from others
e) Analyze and strategize before acting

2. When I feel stressed, my first reaction is usually to:
a) Take action to fix the problem
b) Distract myself with other activities
c) Worry and ruminate about worst-case scenarios
d) Talk about it with someone
e) Try to calm myself through breathing or relaxation

3. Under pressure, my communication style tends to become:
a) More direct or forceful
b) More withdrawn or quiet
c) More emotional or reactive
d) More people-pleasing
e) More analytical or detail-oriented

4. My typical physical response to stress is:
a) Increased energy, restlessness, or agitation
b) Fatigue or a desire to sleep
c) Tension, pain, or physical discomfort

d) Changing eating patterns
e) Difficulty concentrating or mental fog

5. To cope with stress, I most often:
a) Exercise or engage in physical activity
b) Watch TV, browse social media, or engage in other distractions
c) Use substances (caffeine, alcohol, food, etc.)
d) Seek social support
e) Practice mindfulness or relaxation techniques

6. When stressed about a relationship, I tend to:
a) Become confrontational or critical
b) Withdraw or become distant
c) Become clingy or needy
d) Try to resolve the issue through communication
e) Analyze the situation, but hesitate to address it directly

7. My sleep patterns under stress typically:
a) I have trouble falling asleep due to an active mind
b) I sleep more than usual as an escape
c) I wake up during the night and can't get back to sleep
d) My sleep is affected by others' needs or concerns
e) I have vivid dreams or nightmares

8. When facing uncertainty, I usually:
a) Take control and make decisions quickly
b) Avoid thinking about it
c) Worry extensively about possible outcomes
d) Seek reassurance from others
e) Gather information and make contingency plans

Interpretation:
Look for patterns in your responses. Predominant responses in categories:
- Mostly A's: "Fight" stress response - action-oriented, may become aggressive under pressure
- Mostly B's: "Flight" stress response - avoidance-oriented, may disconnect under pressure
- Mostly Cs: "Freeze" stress response - anxiety-oriented, may become paralyzed under pressure
- Mostly D's: "Tend & Befriend" stress response - connection-oriented, seek social support
- Mostly E's: "Analyze" stress response - thinking-oriented, may overthink under pressure

Understanding your typical stress response pattern can help you develop more balanced coping strategies.

5. Values Alignment Assessment

Rate how aligned your current life is with each value (1=completely misaligned, 10=completely aligned):

- Health and Vitality: ______________________________
- Meaningful Work: ______________________________
- Loving Relationships: ______________________________
- Personal Growth: ______________________________
- Contribution/Service: ______________________________
- Financial Well-being: ______________________________
- Creativity and Expression: ______________________________
- Spirituality/Connection: ______________________________
- Play and Joy: ______________________________
- Peace and Serenity: ______________________________

For values scoring six or below, answer:

1. What specific aspects of this value are missing in my life?
2. What small step could I take to bring more alignment?
3. What barriers or beliefs are keeping me from living this value more fully?